Contents

Appendices

Introduction

In the 1980s staff development was associated in most people's minds with central 'service provision', dominated by training workshops, based either in the staffing or personnel department or in an educational unit of some kind. Departments, however, continued to operate largely independently from the centre, and have remained, as they have always been, at the heart of academic life and organisation. Centrally organised staff development has performed some useful functions, but has often had limited success in influencing departmental practice. However, in the late 1990s a range of changes and pressures have emphasised departments as the appropriate focus and source of staff development.

Departments are the 'unit of assessment' for both the Research Assessment Exercise and Subject Review (formerly TQA). The 'self-assessment' which is the first stage of Quality Assessment is often a powerful trigger to staff development – the second trigger being the assessment grading and report itself. In comparison with the extraordinary extent to which these external assessments have affected staff, quality audit of institutions has had little impact on everyday life within departments.

Financial devolution to departments has occurred to a greater or lesser extent. This has confronted many departments, often for the first time, with the financial consequences of many of their decisions and highlighted the need for greater expertise concerning, for example, cost-effective teaching methods. Staff development budgets have often been devolved to departments at the same time, and with them the responsibility to spend these budgets strategically and to report on how effectively they have been spent.

Quality assurance (QA) has been increasingly devolved so that departments have much greater responsibility and autonomy. They may be required to evaluate effectiveness and to use the consequent evaluation evidence to highlight staff development needs. Demands for quality assurance are increasingly complex and rigorous. Departments involved in collaborative/franchised provision of professional and work-based accreditation will have additional responsibilities to support their staff in meeting these QA demands.

Some institutions, such as Oxford Brookes University, have also devolved staffing decisions such as promotion, retaining only loose central monitoring. Departments have often had scope to appoint staff, to certify the satisfactory completion of probation, to approve transfer from Lecturer A to Lecturer B (or from Lecturer II to Senior Lecturer) or to recommend additional increments. Once the department controls the reward and advancement mechanisms in this way there is enormous scope for focused and influential staff development, although this scope is seldom exploited to the full.

Departments have usually had considerable control over the way sabbaticals and study leave are used, even if final approval of decisions lies elsewhere. In many departments study leave provision accounts for 10% of the salaries budget, which would be perceived as an extraordinary 'training' budget, even in a radical modern commercial company.

1 Organisation, policy and responsibility

1.1 Linking departmental with central staff development

The location of funding influences the nature and effectiveness of staff development activity. Traditionally, departments have controlled budgets concerned with scholarship (for conference attendance, sabbaticals and study for higher degrees), while central units have controlled budgets concerned with teaching development, management and personal development, and support staff development. The departmental focus has meant that considerable sums have sometimes been spent on sabbaticals – up to 15% of the university's salary budget – with little concern for centrally determined priorities and with little accountability. The central focus has sometimes meant that university provision has been poorly articulated with departmental needs, and departments have paid scant attention to staff development associated with some of the main areas of operation, such as teaching. At its worst, central provision may consist of isolated topic-based workshops chosen on the basis of superficial needs analyses, attended largely by those who do not need to come. Meanwhile, lecturers struggle with severe everyday work problems which do not consist of neat topics and which require, but do not receive, a solution at department level. Departments have often been critical of the top-slicing of funds for central staff development, while the centre often has little trust in departments' willingness or ability to take staff development seriously should funding be devolved.

The links between central and department-based staff development have often not been fully effective. Patterns of linkage currently in operation include:

- most funding being devolved, but departments being obliged to spend some of this on services provided by a central unit which meets central policy requirements (from fire extinguisher training to courses for new staff linked to probation requirements);

- departments being strongly represented on the committee or board controlling the operation of, or at least responsible for, the central staff development unit;

- individuals within departments being identified as the link persons with the central staff development unit (as at the University of Warwick, for example, where departmental lecturers nominated as academic staff development co-ordinators are important departmental links to centrally organised staff development);

- devolved models in which there is no central unit but only a consortium of departmental staff development personnel (as at the University of Hull, for example, where departments collaborate to run an extended programme for new lecturers leading to SEDA accreditation, entirely through departmental support;

- various versions of internal markets with services delivered by a central unit to departments at full or partial cost, under 'service level agreements', or by allocation of a set volume of centrally funded service to be used as determined by the department, rather than the centre (as at Oxford Brookes University, see over).

Oxford Centre for Staff and Learning Development

Oxford Brookes University

Oxford Brookes used to have an Educational Methods Unit, which was concerned primarily with staff development for teaching and learning, in addition to a modest staff development provision for support staff based within Personnel – neither of which had formal links with departments. Priorities were largely decided centrally or in response to individual approaches. In 1996 all staff development provision at Brookes was reorganised within a single unit, OCSLD. A new form of operation of staff development has been adopted, which places departmental priorities at the centre of planning. All compulsory central demands on staff development are identified – for example, the programme for new lecturers and requirements for appraisal and interview training are built into university policy. All remaining 'service delivery days' available, about 500 in all, are then divided between departments on a pro-rata basis, and each department is allocated a number of days of staff development support which they control. These days are available on a 'use it or lose it' basis. After departments undertake their annual round of strategic planning, a member of OCSLD visits each department and negotiates staff development priorities in relation to their strategic plans.

In this way, while a proportion of the funding for staff development is top-sliced and allocated to a central unit, what this unit does is determined largely by individual departments and their response to strategic planning.

1.2 Formulating departmental staff development policies

It is common for departmental staff development provision to be a patchwork of academic tradition (for example, concerning sabbatical and conference support) and ad hoc initiatives, with limited direction or co-ordination and with a lack of clarity about who is responsible for what, and about how decisions involving funding are made. Increasingly, departments are formalising arrangements within an explicit policy statement which identifies purposes, responsibilities, mechanisms, entitlements, priorities (or values) and main activities, sometimes specified differently for each category of staff. Headings for a model departmental staff development policy are listed overleaf.

Departmental staff development policy framework

CONTEXT

Locating the department within the university and relating staff development to the strategic aims and objectives at institutional and departmental level. Some notion of the origins of the aims and objectives provides a background. This may include reference to items initiating the response (e.g. quality assessment), who is involved (e.g. staff within the department or central quality assurance staff), how it was created and the form of consultation (e.g. Subject Review feedback or course evaluations).

AIMS

The overall intentions of the policy are clearly listed.

OBJECTIVES OR OUTCOMES

A list of statements indicating what the staff development practice will enable the department to do.

PRINCIPLES AND VALUES

Identification of the underpinning beliefs and values informing the policy and driving the allocation of scarce resources. If there are key criteria which determine staff development decisions to be made, these should be made explicit. Relevant entitlement information about the support and development different categories of staff may receive should be included (e.g. full-time staff are entitled to 35 days' study leave, one conference and three days' training per year).

ROLES AND RESPONSIBILITIES

The roles of the key people involved and their responsibilities through a series of activities (e.g. the staff development co-ordinator will provide an annual review of the staff development activity and plans for the HoD). This may include reference to all stakeholders (e.g. lecturers are responsible for identifying their own staff development needs, to make their expertise known and available to colleagues).

STRUCTURE

The mechanisms for achieving the aims and objectives of the policy. The activities involved, who will work with whom and the structures within the institution or department that will facilitate, support and monitor the activities (e.g. teaching observations will be embedded into the department by a one-day workshop, which will be followed by the staff development co-ordinator with two other named persons who will set up small informal working groups to monitor colleagues' experiences of the process and provide specific support as required. The co-ordinator will report back on evaluation findings to the department teaching and learning group).

MONITORING AND EVALUATION

A list of how staff development activities will be monitored and evaluated and the quality assurance process of feeding the information about the effectiveness of the activities back into the departmental decision-making process.

PLAN

During the next three years the department intends to achieve the following aims and objectives. It may be appropriate to set specific targets indicating what will be achieved within a set part of the time period of the plan.

RESOURCING

An indication of the resourcing available to support the policy and how the allocation of resources will be managed.

ACTIVITY 1.1

DEVELOPING YOUR OWN PLAN

Read through the examples of the staff development policies in Appendices I, II, III and IV. As you read through each individual document, identify for yourself the strengths and weaknesses of each document. Once you have read all the appendices, return to the matrix and identify the strengths that you would wish to incorporate in your own document. These are your adoption points. Use the framework above to help you incorporate your adoption points in a policy framework.

Managing Staff Development in Departments: Policy Documents			
	Strengths	Weaknesses	Adoption Points
University of Anon City Division of Professional Practice			
Bath College of HE Faculty of Humanities			
Kingston University Faculty of Technology			
LSU College of HE Faculty of Education			
Your own policy			

1.3 Linking individual staff development to departmental development

Staff development has, until recently, been seen as a personal matter, with individuals identifying their own development interests and needs, often through an appraisal process. The development of the department has often been seen as the sum of the development of its staff. As funding has tightened and strategic and corporate planning have become common, staff development too has become more strategic and departments have tried to use staff development as a vehicle to achieve explicit departmental goals. Sometimes these goals can be expressed in considerable detail in a way which makes staff development

implications clear and unavoidable. In such contexts staff development becomes an adjunct to organisational development rather than a personal matter.

A department must have clear goals so that individual development can be oriented towards them. At Queensland University of Technology each department is required to write a 'Teaching Profile', which is a summary of the teaching rationale of the department: about why particular teaching, learning and assessment methods are used, about the direction of change of these methods and what will be done to achieve consistent and comprehensive change. Appendix V contains an extract from the 'Teaching Profile' of the Law Department from QUT to illustrate the way in which such an explicit statement could orient individual staff development within a department.

As departments are becoming increasingly financially accountable, and the market grows more competitive, they are looking to expand into new areas and diversify provision. The implications for staff development are often significant, as the new developments are often innovative and challenging to members of staff. For example, the accountability and quality assurance mechanisms vary greatly between regional/international franchised courses, teacher training courses, professionally accredited courses and practitioner-based or work-based courses. The same development and support mechanism will not support staff fulfilling all these roles.

The need for clear goals towards which individuals are able to orientate themselves becomes more important as departments embrace change. There is a need for plans to be monitored and reviewed within relatively short time-frames so that any movement in terms of departmental development can be reflected in the staff development planning.

Appendix VI contains an outline of the way a department at the University of Cincinnati planned change, aided by a central until which concentrated exclusively on helping departments to develop such plans.

1.4 Using departmental staff development co-ordinators

It is vital that the person responsible for staff development within departments is clearly identified. Heads rarely have the time, and may not have the expertise or inclination, to give much attention to staff development. It is becoming common to appoint a departmental staff development co-ordinator. It is helpful if the role is carried out by an established, preferably senior, member of staff, since it must entail asking colleagues to review practice. The co-ordinator should have guidance and support and, in particular, a role description, if he or she is to do more than simply keep a record of courses attended. Given the potentially sensitive nature of some of the information involved, issues of confidentiality must be resolved.

A co-ordinator's responsibilities could include:

- formulating a department staff development policy (see 1.2 above) if none exists, and implementing and reviewing it if it does;

- making staff development opportunities (such as courses, funds, expertise) known to colleagues;

- identifying colleagues' interests and development needs through short informal interviews;

- arranging seminars or workshops;

- liaising with a central staff development unit and/or staff development co-ordinators in other departments;

- administering a staff development budget for conferences, courses and expenses associated with staff development activities such as visits and events;

- bidding for staff development funds from the institution or from external sources;

- administering the sabbatical and study leave system;

- reviewing the outcomes of appraisal with the head or chair of department to identify common staff development needs in relation to department strategic plans;

- reviewing student feedback and course evaluation data, or course reports, for issues of common concern which staff development could help to address (see Section 2.2);

- developing and administering a mentor scheme for new staff;

- developing and administering 'succession planning' to induct staff into roles they will take over from colleagues;

- drawing up proposals for staff and staff development changes within the department following major reviews such as Research Assessment and Subject Review (formerly TQA) or review by professional bodies;

- being involved in all departmental appointment, probation, salary and promotion processes and decisions.

Institutions which use staff development co-ordinators can support them with:

- clear specification of expectations;

- meetings with other co-ordinators to share practice;

- opportunities or funding for training in relevant skills (such as running workshops and coaching);

- consultancy, or funds for access to external consultancy, on specific practical issues faced within the department where expertise is not adequate;

- a manual of guidance, elaborating on the points in the list of possible responsibilities above;

- individual mentoring or 'buddying' with an experienced co-ordinator for new co-ordinators in their first year 'in post'.

For large departments, and where co-ordinator roles are extensive, a proper allowance of time should be allocated: half- and even full-time staff development roles within departments are becoming increasingly common.

2 Identifying staff development interests and needs

It is vital to identify needs accurately, but difficult to do so. Methods of analysis may be faulty or poorly applied; communication may be ineffective at various points; and even the individuals involved may not be sure of what they need. There are several possible approaches.

2.1 Using appraisal

Appraisal was originally adopted partly with the aim of identifying staff development needs. However, at the time appraisal was introduced, few departments engaged in active staff development and central staff development units had no access to confidential appraisal documentation. In addition, few departments had the kinds of clear directions, illustrated in Appendices V and VI, which could help to identify ways in which individuals needed to develop to help the department to move in planned directions. Ways of undertaking appraisal have developed almost in a staff development vacuum, and it has not been usual for departmental staff development priorities, or even clear individual development plans, to emerge from appraisal. Furthermore, appraisal has often been backward looking, reviewing individuals' past performance, rather than forward looking, exploring how individuals can contribute more to the achievement of departmental goals. A key question for appraisal is:

'Given the departments' strategic plans, what competencies do staff need to acquire, and what *would be an effective and a congenial way to acquire them*?'

Staff can be asked to think about their staff development needs in advance of their appraisal meeting instead of trying to derive these in retrospect by deduction from their performance.

It is not only the 'content' of staff development needs which should be recorded and collated, but also the preferred methods. Many staff tend to equate staff development with course attendance, and so return a nil response because they cannot think of a course that would meet their needs. It may be that a little private tuition from a more experienced colleague is what is needed. Options for forms of staff development provision can perhaps be listed to prompt discussion at interview, so that a preference is decided upon from a range of possibilities, rather than leaving the means of meeting the need to be determined after the interview. This will serve the dual purpose of increasing the number of needs identified and finding acceptable ways of meeting them.

A collation of expressed staff development interests and preferred methods identified through appraisal may still need to be written up and circulated for reactions and discussion before plans can be adopted with confidence.

2.2 Using course evaluation and review

It is relatively common for course review or student feedback to identify problems, but it is less common for possible solutions or their staff development implications to be identified. In the module report form below, one of the headings to which each module leader is expected to respond concerns staff development implications. Reading a full set of such module report forms could easily identify the priorities for staff development. In this way course review identifies one of the most important agendas for action: the help that people require to overcome the problems identified.

MODULE REPORT FORM

Module title	3501 Introduction to Egyptology
Tutor(s)	T. Khamen
Semester/year	Semester 2 1997/8
No. of students	125
Evaluation agenda	Adequacy of library stocks
Evaluation evidence collected	Standard questionnaire
	Library book usage data
Planning issues to be addressed	The library cannot support reading – learning materials need to be produced
STAFF DEVELOPMENT ISSUES TO BE ADDRESSED	FOUR LECTURERS NEED TRAINING AND TECHNICAL SUPPORT IN LEARNING MATERIALS PRODUCTION
Evaluation agenda for next operation of module	Effectiveness of learning materials

2.3   Using surveys

Most human resource development texts will advise on the use of questionnaires to elicit staff development needs. However, asking individuals to identify personal weaknesses (for that is how questions about staff development needs are interpreted) seldom elicits usable information. Asking staff to tick items from lists of workshop topics seems to have the opposite effect – staff tick far more topics than they are ever likely to commit time to attending. If you still intend to use questionnaires, the following advice may help.

If you have little idea what staff needs are:

* use very open-ended questions;

* avoid eliciting guilt or defensiveness;

* link what staff write to something neutral, such as work practices, rather than personal competence.

EXAMPLES:

Please identify aspects of your current work which are problematic where new working practices might help (e.g. reducing heavy marking loads with new assessment methods using a new email software to cope with the volume of email messages you now send and receive).

Please identify changes which the department is planning which may make demands on you and which your work up until now has not prepared you for (e.g.postgraduate supervision on the proposed MSc, teaching students transferable skills or using a new cataloguing software package).

Where you already have some idea about interests and needs but do not know their extent:

- use closed questions;

- instead of asking for basic information go straight for possible plans;

- offer outline plans and ask people to select, prioritise or amend them to suit personal preferences.

It may be difficult to identify the most appropriate methods of analysis or combination of methods that inform you accurately and efficiently about staff needs. Use the checklist below to identify the processes you have available and the effectiveness they provide. You may be able to identify other methods that you wish to use or develop further.

EXAMPLE:

Which of the following departmental staff development initiatives would you be most likely to commit time and effort to in the next year?

1   Offering individual 'tuition' to others, on demand, on a use of IT with which you are familiar.

     Offer:

2   Taking up others' offers of personal tuition on:

     Communicating via email

     Producing WWW pages

3   Reducing marking loads by changing departmental policies and practices.

4   Using personal tuition to avoid student drop-out

     Comment

IDENTIFICATION OF STAFF DEVELOPMENT NEEDS: CHECKLIST

Gather information about staff development in current practices:

- effectiveness in achieving organisational goals

- effectiveness in achieving personal goals

- future value

Information available:

- Individual requests

- Appraisal interviews

- Student/customer feedback

- Course evaluation

- Audit

- Inspection/review

- Observation (teaching/customer service)

- Management

Others:

3 Identifying and sharing expertise

Much useful staff development comes about informally as individuals consult others who have special expertise they need to tackle specific tasks. If you wanted to know how to obtain a grant from a particular research body you would probably find it much more helpful to talk with someone who was recently successful with that body, or who sits on the selection panel, than to attend a short course about the topic in general. Identifying those with expertise and putting people in touch with each other to share information can be a very effective, cheap and socially acceptable form of staff development.

3.1 Innovations audit

Identifying types of innovation

A sensible first step in developing teaching methods is to find out who is already doing what. An audit of, for example, current assessment methods and practices (how criteria are set and marks allocated, how feedback is given, how students are briefed for exams and project work, and so on) can be a valuable start for staff development about assessment. The most common method is to ask for brief case studies. The SHEFC project on assessment, ASSHE, is a good example of using a simple format to collect and describe cases in print and electronically (Hounsell, 1996). A number of universities produce collections of innovations in teaching, learning and assessment in the form of a publication. At the University of Hull this collection and publication is done through a network of faculty staff development co-ordinators. Some departments, such as Computer Science at Kingston University, do this entirely for themselves, documenting best practice so as to

share it as widely as possible amongst staff.

Such collections are easier within departments because practice is usually less diverse, the scale of the task is more manageable and the examples have obvious contextual relevance and credibility.

Logging frequency and variations

Every department has a range of practice and examples from which its staff can learn. Differences in practice which emerge from audits, but are often assumed not to exist, can intrigue people and engage them in reviewing their own practice in ways general exhortation cannot. An assessment audit could ask individuals what uses of IT in teaching are currently being tried out. Where several people all use, for example, Lotus Notes to create electronic discussion groups, these lecturers could get together to share how they set up and support these discussion groups. Where no use is being made of some practices at all, individuals can see whom to approach for advice on their introduction.

3.2 Expertise databases

Electronic directories

It is a relatively simple matter to mount an electronic directory of expertise available within the department and, ideally, across an institution, either on the worldwide web or using a database that allows searching for topics. You will need a standard format for presenting information (a print-based proforma can be used for technophobes) and a person nominated to look after the database and keep it up to date. The form of expertise available should be as specific as possible and contact information should be provided for direct one-to-one confidential contact. Printed directories can be provided for those who cannot gain electronic access to databases.

It can be difficult to elicit claims of special expertise in the UK academic culture and so prompts may help, such as this example:

EXPERIENCE AND EXPERTISE:
Research bodies from which you have recently succeeded in obtaining funds
Journals for which you have refereed or edited
Software packages you use and could introduce to others
Departmental administrative tasks you have undertaken
Examining and reviewing roles you have performed for other institutions
Other potential useful experience (e.g. dealing with media, sitting on committees)

'Offers' and 'requests'

An elaboration on simple electronic lists is to ask everyone in the department to both offer and request expertise. This makes it less likely that individuals will hide their light under a bushel and acknowledges that most people have both strengths and needs when it comes to expertise.

DR MARY BENFLEET, LECTURER IN ORGANIC CHEMISTRY

OFFERS

- Liaising with overseas university departments to set up franchises and linked courses
- Writing open learning materials
- Using Powerpoint to present visual material in class
- Undergraduate selection interviewing

REQUESTS

- Using www browsers to find things on the net
- Applying for EU funding
- Interviewing prospective mature postgraduate students
- Training my students to use camcorders

SANJAY RAO, ADMINISTRATOR

OFFERS

- Word for Windows 5.0 (including advanced functions such as indexes, footnotes)
- Using the Netscape and www browsers
- Staff selection, drafting job specifications, managing interview panels, associated documentation
- Using video camcorders

REQUESTS

- Time and task management, prioritising
- Setting up an office system for all lecturers' OHPOs (Powerpoint?)
- Office system for storing open learning materials

3.3 Documentation and resource collections

Most lecturers have their own stock of materials containing good ideas derived from years of experience. These may include teaching materials and past research grant applications.

Module handbooks

Many lecturers provide their students with module handbooks, putting a range of handouts together which explain how a module operates and what it contains. But do lecturers know what others provide for their students and how their modules are actually designed to operate? An office collection of all module handbooks is a tremendous staff development resource, and where one exists there tends to be a levelling up of standards until most approach the scale and quality of the best, because it is highly visible if standards vary widely.

Handouts and OHP foils

Some departments are moving away from the traditional notion of lecturers having their own private teaching materials towards common ownership through setting up an electronic database of all handouts used to support teaching, all overhead projector foils and slides used, all exercises and assignments, all laboratory session notes, all case studies and so on, for all courses in the department. A standard format is often established, sometimes including templates and electronic 'style guidelines', and over time all materials are converted into this format. Secretarial or technician support may be required early on until everyone is familiar with the new format and is creating all new material to the new standard. Shared material enables staff to put lectures and courses together much more quickly and allows for more flexibility about who teaches particular sessions or even whole modules. The

expertise resides, to some extent, in the teaching materials, and, if these are shared, so is the expertise.

Exemplary documentation

It is also useful to share and collate, in the departmental office, successful grant proposals, successful sabbatical applications, successful book proposals to publishers, and so on. Lecturers can scan relevant examples and then consult their authors for direct access to the expertise involved. Spreadsheets for costing grant applications or for collating student marks can be mounted on the department's file server as can effective page layouts for teaching materials, exemplary course evaluation reports or student feedback questionnaires.

3.4 Shadowing

'Shadowing' involves observing and working alongside someone who is already doing what you need to learn how to do. It can be a particularly effective way of learning to undertake complex new jobs where there is no easy access to training or written guidance but easy access to experienced practitioners. Examples can include specific duties, such as being deputy head of department, examinations secretary or admissions tutor, but also generic skills, such as chair or secretary of a large committee or team leader for a large research group. Shadowing needs to involve briefing and debriefing as well as observation (e.g. discussion before and after a key meeting as well as during the meeting) and also 'Sitting by Nellie', asking questions while a task is in hand (e.g. sifting through student application forms or scrutinising exam results for a series of courses, looking for potential problems). Shadowing uses relatively little of the expert's time and relatively little 'coaching' expertise other than being open and prepared to answer questions.

Some universities and departments have an organised 'succession planning', in which the next person to carry out a complex task or duty is identified well in advance so as to allow a period of shadowing and learning about the job before they takes over. In some contexts such shadowing is compulsory.

Sometimes there is no one in your own department doing the job to be shadowed (though the kind of databases outlined above would make such expertise easier to find), and shadowing might then involve others in other departments or even other institutions. Shadowing can also allow 'understudies' to take over key roles if illness or extended leave intervene.

3.5 Peer review of courses and teaching

Observation

One of the best ways to improve is to have someone observe you and give feedback on how you perform. Observing others is also valuable. Subject Review involves observation of classes, and it is helpful to have experienced being observed and to know about potential weaknesses others are likely to spot. But it is also important to distinguish between observation for the purpose of making judgements and what we are suggesting here: observation to provide formative feedback and support individuals in reflecting on and developing their own practice. The most effective arrangements for observation of teaching, for the purposes of staff development, have the following characteristics:

- they are confidential: nothing of what takes place is discussed with others;

- information is used for no other purpose, especially not for appraisal or promotion;

- they are reciprocal: two people observe each other's teaching and have a vested interest in fairness, neutrality and confidentiality;

- they are focused on description as a way of developing realistic self- awareness, not judgement, and training or at least clear guidelines are necessary to limit unacceptable slippage into subjective value judgement.

Muddling up concerns for accountability, or the need to monitor or judge staff, with concerns for development will inevitably compromise or even stop the development and lead to 'faking good'. In ideal circumstances a lecturer would invite a colleague in for a (reciprocal) observation to a class where there were problems which needed to be addressed, where the colleague's perceptions might be useful. Observation for judgement is usually of a 'best' class where little could be learnt. Some institutions have compulsory peer observation schemes with training for all in how to observe and give feedback. Appendices IX and X offer detailed guidance on institutional peer observation schemes which could form the basis of a department scheme.

3.6 Linking with other departments and central staff development

Pooling expertise and running collaborative workshops

At the University of Guelph in Canada the central educational development centre had a policy of never running workshops for departments. They would only ever run such events with them on a collaborative basis, sharing expertise, sharing planning, sharing presentations and so on. This acknowledged and mobilised the expertise already embedded within the department. The general principle here is clear: don't just invite experts in to operate as if the department knew nothing and had nothing to offer. Use workshops and consultancies as much to elicit and share expertise within the department as to buy in expertise from outside.

Reciprocal workshops and consultancy

Departments are often sufficiently expert in a range of fields to be able to mount workshops for each other. One science department may have reorganised its laboratory programme while another may have developed the worldwide web to deliver all student handouts. They could easily run workshops for each other on a reciprocal basis, just as it is suggested below that they can usefully reciprocally evaluate each others' modules or courses. At the University of Hull educational development is organised on a collaborative basis between faculties, with no central educational development unit, and much sharing of this kind occurs.

Much educational and staff development consultancy is of a generic nature – the consultant uses consultancy skills to help clarify the problem, helps identify options for tackling it, helps evaluate the options and then helps plan their implementation. Many people within departments have some of these consultancy skills associated with other aspects of their work, and can use them to help other departments (but not their own, because prophets have no honour in their own land!). It is possible, however, for departments to offer reciprocal consultancy. An accountancy department can offer to consult on the financial system and what the office staff need to learn to do to improve it, and the other, in return, can offer to consult on economising on the assessment system and what accountancy staff need to learn to change assessment methods.

Audits of expertise (see 3.1) help to identify where such reciprocal consultancies may be possible, but the role of specific expertise should not be overestimated – managing the consultancy process is just as important.

Joint events

Many problems faced by departments and the skills gaps they need to bridge are common to other departments. For example, almost everyone is faced with resource problems and understaffing and almost everyone needs more IT awareness and skills. When departments come together to share an event on the same topic this can greatly increase learning through sharing ideas and expertise, through recognising similarities and differences and by getting a more detached perspective on your own problems. We also suspect that staff within departments behave themselves much better in the company of others from other departments, perhaps ashamed of revealing the infighting, rivalries, ritual cynicism and stifling hierarchies which can block change within a department.

3.7   Mentoring

Mentoring involves providing someone who is new to a job or role access to a person more experienced at that role, for guidance, advice and feedback. In many departments, as a matter of formal policy, both academic and support staff have their own mentor until probation has been completed. Many programmes for new lecturers, for example, at the universities of Keele and Nottingham, involve a mentor to provide subject-relevant teaching support within a department. Often the most appropriate person to perform such a mentoring role is not someone senior and highly expert but someone with recent experience of learning the job. For new lecturers the best mentor is often a lecturer of similar age who has been through the programme for new lecturers within the last couple of years. Empathy and minimum status and seniority differences are usually more important than absolute levels of expertise. Relevant expertise is useful, however, and a lecturer might need a research mentor as well as a teaching mentor, as it is not easy to find one person able to fulfil both roles well.

A mentor may meet the new person right at the start, have occasional scheduled meetings throughout the first year initiated by the mentor, and more frequent unscheduled informal meetings initiated by the new member of staff. A mentor may be expected to observe teaching, discuss course plans, check exam questions and double-mark some assignments, getting as close as possible to the everyday details of teaching in a way which an end-of-year review could not do. The mentor might be expected to provide practical support (about regulations, the availability of services, and so on) and be a personal support, short of anything requiring counselling. A mentor is not a line manager, however; the more formal roles associated with probation, appraisal and allocation of duties are best not handled by the mentor.

Often individuals adopt a range of duties of increasing scale and complexity as they gain experience, and a different mentor may be appropriate for each new level of responsibility. In the School of Business at Oxford Brookes University, new teaching staff of all kinds have a separate mentor for their first teaching within a module, then for taking responsibility for running a single module, then for running a year of the course, and so on. The taking on of all new major responsibilities is supported by a mentor, and the intention is that no one takes on significant new responsibilities without an identified person for support.

Appendices VII and VIII outline mentoring schemes at the universities of Durham and Hull respectively.

3.8   Visits

It is often assumed that if a department or an individual has a problem then a workshop or short course is the best way to tackle it. However, a visit to somewhere that has tackled and solved the problem already might be much more cost-effective. Seeing alternative teaching methods in action or a different way of organising an office or laboratory, and talking to those involved, can make a considerable impact. Paying for four staff each to visit a different place and report back on what they have learnt can generate more ideas than all four going on the same course. And a whole department, or a group within a department, such as the office staff or laboratory staff, going on a visit together can have a much greater impact on their collective approach to change than if a consultant or trainer came to run a session for them.

4 Running seminars and workshops

One of the most common failures of staff development involves the workshop no one turns up to on a topic no one is interested in, or at least which no one believes would be useful at that time or in that format. Individual needs, identified in surveys or interviews, may have been pooled in a way which generalises and decontextualises from specific interests until staff do not even recognise their own interests in the titles of workshops. Well-targeted events in departments can avoid this problem.

4.1 Lunchtime seminars

A seminar may enable the informal sharing of how people are tackling teaching and assessment problems and trying out new methods.

In a very informal way one or two people might describe a modest innovation in teaching they are trying, in the format:

- this is what I used to do

- this was the problem

- these are the options I considered

- this is what I actually did

- this is what happened

- this is what I am going to do next

- if you were going to copy me, the advice I would give is

The seminar can be written up on one side of A4 and circulated. Summaries may be collected in a folder for reference. Departmental funds might be used for coffee and sandwiches at one or two such events each term.

4.2 Running workshops

Workshops provide an opportunity for staff to share ideas and to solve problems, usually through exploring and applying practical skills. They are particularly useful for developing expertise in activities that involve interpersonal skills, since learning by experience is usually the most effective approach in such areas, and workshops can allow the simulation of real situations.

It is possible to make a workshop very open and flexible. Its purpose might be to generate ideas about how problems identified by participants might be solved.

There is a danger that discussion may become merely anecdotal and not establish principles for practice. Some participants may not be used to the idea of deriving theory from practice, and may see it as either 'the pooling of ignorance' or 'telling ourselves what we know anyway'. The phrase 'share ideas' reduces some to apoplexy. The workshop leader has a part to play here in injecting 'theory' at appropriate points. This might take the form of definitions, concepts, frameworks, research findings and so on. It might be simply a matter of allowing a few minutes for the group to agree on DOs and DON'Ts that they feel have arisen from activity and discussion. This can be prompted by asking participants individually to note down three key points or to complete the sentence: 'A person engaged in X should . . .' and then gathering in the answers.

EXAMPLE

TOPIC

Half-day workshop on encouraging group discussion. The workshop invites participants to explore their own problems and suggest solutions and deals with questioning techniques that can promote student contributions to discussion.

PROGRAMME

1400	Introduction
1405	Participants asked individually to note three key problems for them of dealing with discussion in groups.
1410	Problems gathered on board/flipchart. Common themes identified.
1420	Participants work in pairs or small groups, taking several of the problems and generating possible solutions.
1450	Solutions presented to whole group on OHTs.
1510	Presentation on questioning technique, focusing on open and exploratory questioning.
1530	Tea
1545	Pairs generate open and closed questions on a topic which might be discipline-specific or general, depending on the group.
1555	Questions reported back to group, gathered for display.
1605	Triad exercise, where one participant tries to engage the other two in discussion, first by asking closed questions with the intention of preventing discussion developing, and then by open questioning techniques. The others should be trying to contribute at all times. Debrief, and exchange roles, repeating the process.
1645	Report back to main group, summarising any principles or DOs and DON'Ts that have been highlighted.
1700	Close

Role play

Often role play will be appropriate. This is a technique that needs introducing with care, as some staff enjoy it whilst others find even the prospect daunting. It is perhaps best to lead it gently. Often a workshop leader will start with a written case study, asking for participants' views on how to solve a problem.

> e.g.: Several staff have expressed concern about the quality of work produced by one of your personal tutees. Various explanations, all of them alarming and all based on guesswork, have been advanced. From your own knowledge of the student you believe that heavy-handed intrusion might be counter-productive.

> What action would you take, and what factors would you take into account in deciding what to do?

When participants have talked through a case study, they might then be asked to suggest an appropriate way of opening a tutorial session. They might follow this by predicting what the student's response might be.

> e.g.: You have decided to broach the matter with the student. What would your opening comment be?

> What response is this likely to prompt?

It is then a small step to asking pairs of participants to take the roles of tutor and tutee and to role-play the opening minute of the interview.

4.3 Buying in expertise and consultants

A consultant may be used in a number of ways. Sometimes it is useful to bring new ideas into a department, to suggest that there are alternatives, and that others work differently elsewhere. A consultant may offer ideas. Alternatively, a consultant may offer a framework for discussion, or may be used simply as a catalyst for review or development that has been planned by members of the department. Sometimes a consultant can be useful as a politically neutral figure who can encourage groups of people to look afresh at views and ways of working to which they may have become attached. Departments develop traditions concerning what is talked about. There may be a tendency to deal with transactional day-to-day matters (how are we going to staff next term's courses?) but not to address more fundamental issues (what are we trying to achieve in our undergraduate programme?). A consultant can help the department to 'change gear' and focus on other issues.

Obvious rules apply. Staff will not take kindly to a consultant who appears to have been hired to promote the views of a particular person within the department, or whose role has not been made clear at the start. The nature and destination of any intended outcomes of the consultancy should also be known.

The personality of the consultant is clearly an important factor, and it is wise to look for recommendations of suitable consultants from people who have direct experience of using one.

Some will look for a consultant from outside their own institution. This may be politically less sensitive, but may lead to suggestions that the outsider will not understand 'how we do things here'. On the other hand, a consultant may have value precisely because he or she can stand outside the institution's or department's culture.

4.4 Planning and running 'away days'

Committees provide poor opportunities for debate of crucial issues and creative tackling of problems. Working parties or individual work to tackle problems may fail to involve everyone or gain everyone's commitment to solutions or changes.

An away day helps to get everyone together away from office pressures for a short time in order co-operatively to address a shared problem (such as increased student numbers, diverse intake, volume of postgraduate supervision) or an upcoming challenge (such as quality assessment, course revalidation).

You may want to inject some factual material. For instance, if the department has not looked at transferable skills and their integration in the curriculum, then some definition of terms can be useful, and examples of how it has been done elsewhere. However, the purpose of the away day is to get people talking together, so too much passive receiving of information should be avoided. Short briefing notes can be provided beforehand, referred to at the start and used as working documents at appropriate points.

- DO   have a clear purpose for the away day.
- DO   try to make it enjoyable as well as productive.
- DO   achieve and record some clear outcomes.
- DO   make it possible for everyone to play a part.
- DO   ensure that activities are varied.
- DO   allow plenty of space for discussion.
- DO   prepare participants in advance.
- DON'T stay on campus or participants will be called away.
- DON'T use all the time for information-giving.
- DON'T forget to do something with the outcomes!

5 Focusing staff development around quality assurance

The links in institutions between quality assurance and quality enhancement are not always as direct as they should be. Commonly the two issues are dealt with separately, through different committees. However, if quality assurance is to be more than a record of good practice, it must be linked to policies at appropriate levels within the institution which clearly state the contribution of staff development in enhancing the quality of teaching and achieving institutional strategic objectives. It must also make clear the resourcing, the entitlements of different staff groups, the responsibilities of all parties, and how the effectiveness of the activities will be monitored. Clearly staff will be more convinced about the value of spending time on quality assurance procedures if they see that they lead to improvement. Similarly, staff development is made more effective if it is linked with quality assurance. It provides an opportunity to find out in a systematic way what is needed for improvement. Bringing the two together can avoid some duplication of effort.

5.1 Using evaluation of courses and teaching

A great deal of formal and informal evaluation of teaching now takes place routinely. The task of staff development is to make sure that the 'feedback loop' is closed, so that any required improvements are made. Often the loop is closed in terms of meeting quality assurance requirements, but the link to staff development planning is usually missed because the two systems are not embedded. If course evaluations are to be used as a way of linking the two activities, then evaluation planning must take into account the information and evidence required to inform both quality assurance and staff development planning. It is potentially problematic to assume that the two will be the same. The course unit report form (below) provides an example of a simple approach that links the requirements for quality assurance and staff development in a focused, user friendly way.

Student feedback

Many departments have standardised the process of obtaining student feedback, usually through questionnaires; others recommend the practice to staff but do not attempt to standardise. In the latter case, a staff developer can encourage the use of feedback by finding and publicising examples of good practice, by publishing guidelines, by circulating examples of questionnaires and other approaches to evaluation, by running a session for members of the department to share their current practice, and so on. Where a means of obtaining student feedback is properly in place, its effectiveness can be enhanced by ensuring that consideration of student feedback and responses to it are discussed during appraisal and during course and programme team meetings.

Monitoring reports

Departmental activity is now extensively reported on. Systems that require periodic module or course reports are widely in use. Usually, they will refer to any staff development needs or other changes that are required. A staff developer can usefully check through these reports to pick out topics that need to be dealt with. Similarly, where there are staff–student course committees in place, agendas and minutes may provide some suggestions of staff development needs.

Course Unit Report Form

Course Title : Introduction to Archaeology

Evaluation agenda

Programme level: Library problems, student reading.

Course level: Last year there was a problem with students' access to archived documents in the special collection in the library, the consequent volume of reading was insufficient to support the discussion sessions.

Evaluation data collected

Lending data from the library: two evaluation discussion meetings with students undertaken by the educational development unit; short questionnaire about reading and preparation for discussion sessions given to 25% of students.

Evaluation conclusion

The new library skills sessions were well attended and library use and lending rates have increased, but there is still too much comprtition for access to key documents and students still attend session ill-prepared.

Action to be taken

The Department should review the policy on the production of its own learning materials and try to tackle library and reading problems and allocate resources for printing, copyright and secretarial support.

Development needs

Advice on how to prepare learning packages. Time to do this.

Running discussion sessions with adequately prepared students.

Evaluation agenda for next year

Adequacy of learning packages; effect on student use of the library and preparation for discussion sessions.

Example taken from Gibbs G, (1996) Supporting Educational Development within Departments in IJAD pp. 27-37 1, 1

5.2 Using the Research Assessment Exercise and Subject Review (formerly TQA)

Staff developers can help departments to prepare for, undergo and follow up Subject Reviews. Indeed, some universities centre much of their staff development activity on the Review process. At the University of Newcastle, for example, the Quality Enhancement Unit works closely with departments throughout the process. A similar approach can be taken within departments.

Using QA criteria to form an agenda

QAA publishes extensive documentation concerning Review purposes and processes. This includes sets of issues based upon the six aspects of provision that are to be assessed. This can form a very convenient agenda so that a department can consider the extent to which it is working effectively in all of those areas – and is able to demonstrate it. The knowledge in the department that these issues will be the basis of assessment is a considerable motivator.

Shadowing another department being visited

Review takes place over a six-year cycle, during which all departments will be visited. This means that in a large institution there will be several visits in any year. It should therefore be possible to learn from the experience of others who are undergoing the process. The visit itself will be a sensitive time, when members of the department in question will be feeling stressed and, perhaps, not primarily concerned with helping others. However, the period before the assessment may offer opportunities to see how that is being handled. It might be possible to sit in on department meetings, or to find out how the department is preparing its staff for teaching observation. It is particularly useful to see the documentation that is produced, both the self-assessment that must be prepared some months beforehand and the material that is supplied in a base room for assessors during the visit. It is helpful to know how another department has set out its base room, to gauge the extent, organisation and ease of access of information presented.

Visiting departments rated excellent (or 23/24)

Highly rated departments might be very pleased to talk to others about how they have achieved their status. Such a discussion might include not only the way in which the Review process has been managed but also the characteristics and ways of working of the department that have led to such a high score being awarded.

Using the Subject Review report

Assessors produce a report after each visit, commenting on all of the aspects of provision. Strengths are noted and areas for improvement are listed. It is useful to pick up and respond to the latter before the momentum of Review has gone.

Using national Subject Review reports

An overview report is published on each of the disciplines assessed. It identifies the strengths and weaknesses seen by assessors across all visits. It can be very helpful to read the overview reports of other disciplines in advance of the visit to your own department, as a further means of examining existing departmental practice to see how it is likely to be viewed. In due course the overview report of one's own department will help to locate it within the range of practice nationally and may suggest areas for improvement.

5.3 Using observation of teaching

The observation of teaching can be a very effective way of developing expertise, both in the person observed and in the observer. The essentials of organising a teaching observation are not complicated, provided some simple common sense rules are followed (see Appendix X). It is important, however, to be clear about the purpose of the observation. A distinction should be made between developmental and judgemental approaches. In practice the two often shade into each other, but it is as well to be clear about what is to be observed, how, if at all, it is to be recorded, and what will happen afterwards. Ground rules about confidentiality are important.

Peer observation

Many institutions and departments have introduced peer observation, in which pairs of colleagues view each other's sessions and then provide feedback. The process and outcomes are not usually shared beyond the two participants, and this helps to ensure an open atmosphere and an honest sharing of concerns. A reciprocal arrangement helps to keep the observers' feet firmly on the ground and to make sure that the feedback process is managed tactfully. Peer observation is commonly introduced as part of preparations for Review. See Appendix XI for an example of a peer observation report form.

Observation for probation and promotion

Many universities now expect candidates to participate in a programme of teaching and learning prior to successful completion of probation. This practice will be formalised under the Institute of Learning and Teaching, where all new academic staff will be required to complete successfully an accredited award in the area of teaching and learning. An integral part of this programme may be the direct observation of teaching, which will be presented as evidence of their performance. Whilst having a judgemental aspect, it is important to offer the opportunity for the development of individual practice. This can be achieved only if the two aspects, or functions, are kept separate. One way of doing so is to give the candidate the right to submit whatever evidence he or she wishes in support of a claim. The outcomes of a particular observation are included at the discretion of the candidate. Judgements about proficiency or excellence are made on the summative evidence as a whole, which may be in the form of a portfolio, and not on the teaching observation visit alone. Thus the visit can be developmental and yet generate useful evidence on which judgements can be made.

Many universities are developing promotion routes or rewards on the basis of teaching excellence. In some institutions reward is on the basis of promotion in the form of a readership (for example); in others rewards in the form of bursaries or prizes are available.

Departments within institutions who have these routes in place should enable individual members of staff to take the opportunity to gain recognition if they so wish. Enabling staff through a variety of mechanisms should be built into staff development policy and strategic planning and should not be based solely on the ad hoc demands of one or two members of staff.

Observation for appraisal

Appraisal now frequently includes consideration of evidence drawn from direct observation of teaching. The suggestions above may be equally applicable. There is wide agreement that appraisal should be developmental if it is to be of greatest value. Observers can be encouraged to make suggestions concerning further improvements of practice. These can form part of the appraisal discussion and become some of the development aims identified for the individual.

6 Educational development as staff development

6.1 Development projects

There has been major growth in education development activity in higher education in recent years, in part stimulated by the Enterprise in Higher Education initiative, but increasingly carried out by a growing body of academic staff who see that there is value and satisfaction in developing their own practice. Much development and review of teaching, learning and assessment practice has taken place. Such activity almost inevitably means that staff involved gain new skills, and so it is an effective form of staff development.

Departmental priorities for development

It is both a strength and a weakness of educational development that the driving force is often individuals' enthusiasm. Any substantial project consumes limited resources, most commonly in the form of expensive academic time. The work must therefore be carefully targeted, taking several factors into account. The department as a whole should have a clear sense of where it is heading with its teaching and learning approaches, and be identifying any aspects of practice that need such development. Project planning should consider the educational soundness of the central idea, the resources that are required and the benefits that will accrue. This may involve some hard-headed decisions about whether the development is necessary or only desirable, the extent of the impact, in terms of numbers of students affected, the usefulness of the development if applied to other courses or programmes, the opportunity cost of the other activities that will not be resourced as

a result, and so on. The department must be supportive, particularly those who will be involved in changed practice.

Development planning

Academics often find the preparation of detailed funding bids an annoying chore, but the processes of coming to a clear understanding of what exactly it is that is planned and communicating it are valuable ones. A concise statement of aims, objectives, processes, outcomes and resources required, and evaluation strategy, together with a time plan, will not only convince other members of the department that it is a worthwhile investment, but it will also help to shape the work of the project and increase the likelihood of its success. On the basis of this, sensible judgements can be made about the amount of time that should be allocated to the project and any other forms of resourcing that are required.

Central funding

Many universities make development funding available for approaches to teaching and learning. The University of Warwick and the University of Southampton, for example, regularly fund departmental projects through a Teaching Development Fund, to which bids may be submitted by members of staff with departmental support. Where such funding is available, departments should be actively applying, maximising the chances of success through some of the planned approaches suggested above and by consulting other departments to see if there are common needs that could be met through joint work. Other departments will also be receiving funding and developing approaches that might be transferable. It is therefore worth reviewing funded projects regularly for their applicability.

National funding

There are a number of sources of funding for

educational development. The Teaching and Learning Technology Programme (TLTP) funds IT-related development (http://www.tltp.ac.uk/tltp). The Fund for the Development of Teaching and Learning (FDTL) has a wider remit, and funds may be bid for by departments that are particularly successful in Teaching Quality Assessment. Once again it is worth monitoring such activity, to see whether work is being sponsored that may be of use. IT-based development is disseminated in part through discipline-based CTI centres (http://www.cti.ac.uk/) and cross disciplinary Teaching and Learning Support Network Centres (TLTSNs) (http://www.tltp.ac.uk/tltsn/). Charitable bodies, such as the Leverhulme Trust, also sometimes express a willingness to fund educational development work.

There is likely to be someone in the university who has responsibility for identifying sources of educational development funding and ensuring that the university bids appropriately. This may well be within an educational development centre or staff development unit. It is worth making sure that your interest in development is known about, as there is an inevitable matching of bidding opportunities with projects that departments in the university want to undertake.

6.2 Researching practice and publishing

Journals concerned with teaching and learning

There is a growing number of journals, some of a generalist nature and others subject-specific. These include:

- Association for Learning Technology Journal
- Educational Action Research
- Innovation and Learning in Education: The International Journal for the Reflective Practitioner

- Innovations in Education and Training International
- Journal of Further and Higher Education
- Qualitative Studies in Education
- Studies in Higher Education
- Teaching in Higher Education

Most of the above welcome articles from practitioners as well as educational researchers.

There are also journals that are discipline-related, such as:

- British Journal of Music Education
- Educational Studies in Mathematics
- European Journal of Engineering Education
- International Journal of Science Education
- International Journal of Technology and Design Education
- International Research in Geographical and Environmental Education
- Journal of Aesthetic Education
- Journal of Art and Design Education
- Journal of Biological Education
- Journal of Geography in Higher Education
- Physics Education
- Research in Drama Education
- Research into Science and Technological Education

In addition, the Staff and Educational Development Association (SEDA) produces the New Academic, containing short items produced in the main by lecturers.

Conferences concerned with researching practice

There is a growing number of annual conferences in the UK focusing on teaching and learning. Some are specifically aimed at staff and educational developers, but there is a strong move towards teaching and learning being the focus of discipline- and professional-based conferences. Once again, the university's educational development centre or staff development unit may be the best local source of information on these.

7 Staff development within departmental meetings

Departmental meetings are often the only time members of a department get together, but, despite their potential, such meetings are rarely used for staff development. The two simple mechanisms reported below can work to share staff development information and to raise the profile of staff development and help establish a culture of sharing of expertise, both offering and requesting staff development support.

7.1 Reporting staff development and sharing expertise

Some departments list papers published by staff within the department, and grants obtained, in an appendix to departmental agendas or minutes. It can be helpful to go further and report short courses and conferences people have recently attended and to give the people concerned one minute to say something about them. A ten-minute slot is usually enough to make cover this.

7.2 Agenda item

Problem identification

It can be useful to allow a short slot in departmental meetings to identify shared problems which staff might benefit from working on collaboratively.

Offers

'I've just come back from a brilliant workshop on X and I'd be happy to talk through the accompanying materials with anyone interested. I'll put a copy of the materials in the department resource file.'

'At a meeting in London last week I got hold of a copy of the documents for the next round of Research Council funding. Anyone considering applying by the deadline of the end of next month can discuss their outline plans with me if they'd like some feedback.'

'You may remember that last term we discussed the use of posters to assess the outcome of the 2nd-year projects. The posters will be displayed in the main lab all next week if you'd like to have a look and see what happened. The formal presentations are on Thursday, all day, if you'd like to drop in.'

'Mary offered to show us how to use Powerpoint at the last meeting. I took her up on her offer and I'm finding it really helpful. I've mastered how to transfer Word files without losing all the layout and various other tricks if anyone wants a hand.'

'I've got audio tapes of the talks asterisked on the AAHE conference programme going round if you want to listen to any in your car going home. The Seldin one is really interesting.'

Requests

'Can someone who uses the video microscope set-up give me a demo, as I need to use it in a lecture next week?'

'My in-tray is in a mess. Does anyone have a filing system or other way of keeping paperwork under control?'

'I have agreed to run a conference for a group of about 80 people next year and I've never run a conference before. I'd like someone who has experience of doing this to act as a kind of 'mentor' to me throughout the process for advice and to make sure I don't drop anything.'

'I started using project teams this term in my module and the students don't seem to have a clue how to get things done co-operatively. Is there anyone who has used group work like this who can perhaps run a seminar with me with the students or who knows of a good booklet or manual on the topic?'

'I've decided to try putting all my lecture notes on the web so the students can get access to them if they miss the lecture and for the overseas students whose own note-taking is poor. I need technical advice on using html and specific things like security because I don't want other universities stealing my notes. Can anyone help?'

'Is anyone going to the AAHE conference, because I can't, but I'd like several of the papers.'

8 Supporting new staff

8.1 Induction

All new staff, whether probationary or experienced, can be helped to settle in. It is sometimes hard for someone who has been in a department for some years to remember how difficult and confusing the first few weeks in a new job can be. Some of the questions that need answering may be very simple indeed (see the list below). The components of an induction will range from the social to the technical and can form the basis of an induction programme, large or small.

Questions new staff frequently ask

. . . about safety, health and welfare

What do I do if the alarm bell goes?

Who is the departmental safety officer? first aid person?

How do I report accidents? safety hazards?

Where can I go to lie down quietly?

. . . about the rules

Are there rules about special clothing, e.g. lab coats?

Are there rules about recording the handing in of work?

Are there rules about behaviour?

If I want to make a formal complaint, e.g. about harassment, a student, my head of department, how do I go about it?

. . . about teaching

How do I book/change teaching rooms?

Is it possible to make timetable changes? How?

How do I get messages to all my students?

How do I book audio-visual equipment?

Who do I phone when the OHP bulb blows?

How can I get slides made up?

. . . about research

Is there money? How is it allocated?

Who do I bid to for internal funds? How do I get the forms? What are the deadlines? Who can I talk to about it?

. . . about the job

Am I on probation? What, in practice, does this mean?

What are my conditions of service in terms of contact hours? holidays?

How does the institution enforce them?

Just how secure am I? What are my rights in employment? What is the institution's record on compulsory redundancy?

What are the pension arrangements, and are there alternatives, e.g. opting out?

If I have non-academic problems who can I go to outside my department?

How do I 'get on'?

. . . about money

How is my salary calculated?

When is pay day?

How am I paid?

How do I claim for travel expenses? reimbursement of fees, petty cash, etc.?

Can I do consultancy and keep all the fee? Do I need to get permission?

. . . about day-to-day things

Where do I get supplies of chalk, stationery, etc.?

What access is there to computer terminals? word processing? secretarial support?

How to I get reprography, e.g. class handouts?

What's the turn-round time for regular copies?

What's my total reprographics budget?

. . . about courses

How do I find out about the syllabus?

How fixed is it?

Is there a reading list for my courses?

Can I modify them if I want to?

How do I find out about deadlines for setting exams, submission of assignments, sending marks to the office, etc.?

Is there an induction course for students? What is my role in it?

. . . about the library

What's the name of my subject librarian ? tutor librarian?

What can I ask them to do for me? literature searches? student guides? reserve collections?

. . . about administration

What admin do I have to do for the courses I'm responsible for?

Who can tell me how to do admin jobs?

. . . about support

Is there anyone here (e.g. a mentor) who is responsible for me or for my probation or tenure?

Who can help me with my teaching?

How do I find out about courses in lecturing methods?

. . . about the future

How can I find out if the institution/faculty/department has plans for the future which will affect my career decisions?

Can I go on courses I'm interested in?

How often will I get a sabbatical or study leave?

How do I get promotion/ additional increments?

. . . about my husband/wife/partner/family

Is there a staff club or staff association or senior common room, and is my partner automatically a member?

Can my partner use the library/sports/social facilities?

Is there a creche? a nursery?

. . . about sport and recreation

What staff facilities/teams are there?

Can staff use the facilities of the student union?

. . . about social life

Where do people meet for coffee or a beer after work?

Does everyone go home at 5 p.m. or are there lots of things going on in the evenings?

Do I get a list of everyone's name, home address and telephone number?

. . . about domestic matters

Where are the toilets?

Where is the nearest coffee machine?

Is there a sick bay, rest room doctor or nurse anywhere on campus?

. . . about important people

Who are they?

Who is in the office either side of mine?

Few departments are large enough to support a formal induction programme, and it is doubtful in any case whether that is the most effective way of offering help. However, there should be a person who is responsible for inducting each new member of staff, and who may formally be designated as a mentor (see 3.7). He or she should expect to spend some time on this, and it should be clear to the new member of staff that it is acceptable to make use of the time.

8.2 Linking central induction courses to the department

Many universities offer an induction programme to new staff, and this is likely to be compulsory for probationers. There may be an introduction to the university itself, to teaching and learning, to library and computing facilities, and so on. Such provision can be useful, but it cannot of course deal with department-specific issues, and many questions will still need answers. It is helpful, to avoid duplication, if the departmental induction takes account of what is being done at institutional level. This link is sometimes fostered through the role of a mentor or, as at the

University of Southampton, by an appointed senior colleague, who will attend part of the induction session and facilitate sessions within the department.

8.3 Information and documentation

There is a strong tradition in higher education for lecturers to produce their own materials and to organise their work without a great deal of formal documentation. Of course this is rapidly changing. Increasing emphasis on quality assurance means that more is set down on paper. Modularisation requires staff to know more about others' courses and to work within common frameworks. The job of making information readily available is thus easier than it used to be, but it still requires an effort. A departmental resources area, even if it is only a shelf or two in a staff room, can contain valuable materials, such as student handbooks, prospectuses, copies of regulations, syllabuses, and so on. As noted earlier, teaching materials are increasingly shared, and copies of handouts, OHTs and session plans can be held centrally, either for use or to serve as examples.   Many departments make extensive use of video materials, slides and other audio-visual aids. Often these are locked away in the room of the person who is most strongly attached to them! When they are pooled and, more importantly, catalogued, they can be accessed by everybody. The most effective and secure way of making a great deal of material available may be through a web site.

It is easy to gather so much material that the potential user is confused by the quantity of it. A staff handbook is useful, for established as well as new staff, to bring together the key items of information. Some of the contents will be obvious, but, as a guide, it may be worth asking a sample of staff what they really need to know or what they recently found out only with a great deal of effort.

8.4 Periodic reviews

Probation may be three to five years down the road for a lecturer, and this means that intermediate reviews may be helpful. The line manager may need at least a meeting a year, resembling an appraisal interview, specifically oriented to coping with formal probation requirements. If there is a mentor, then more frequent intermediate reviews of a more formative kind may be more supportive. Often such reviews are focussed largely around action planning – what to do next – rather than around staff development – what competences need to be acquired next and what staff development resources and sources of support and expertise are available. New staff are often very willing to put time into learning new skills, and professional development habits established early on may persist.

9 Developing part-time staff

9.1 Specifying entitlements

The general purpose policy for part-time teachers below distinguishes between three types of PT teachers and provides different entitlements and support for each. Much of this policy concerns briefing and support facilities rather than training.

POLICY FOR DEVELOPMENT AND SUPPORT OF PT TEACHERS

1 Each school employing PT teachers should identify a part-time teacher co-ordinator responsible for ensuring that all PT teachers have access to facilities and support to which they are entitled.

2 Occasional and guest teachers should be entitled to:

2.1 a copy of the relevant course documentation describing the course to which they are contributing;

2.2 information concerning optional training opportunities for PT teachers which they have the right to attend;

2.3 student feedback or feedback from a FT teacher.

3 In addition, all PT teachers undertaking more than 50 hours teaching a year should be entitled to:

3.1 access to word processing, email, computer centre and library facilities;

3.2 shared desk space with an internal phone line;

3.3 an induction to the university, to their school and to the logistics of teaching support facilities such as booking and using AV equipment, print-room facilities, pooled room booking;

3.4 a briefing by a named teacher responsible for the course on which they teach and ongoing access to that teacher for guidance and information;

3.5 three days (24 hours) of initial training in teaching, organised by the school (with or without support from staff development), supported by manuals, books or other reference material on teaching;

3.6 the equivalent of one day (8 hours) of ongoing training each year (with or without support from staff development);

3.7 observation of teaching by an experienced teacher within the first year of teaching;

3.8 feedback from students on teaching;

3.9 a copy of information available to FT teachers, such as course evaluations and student performance evidence, which could assist the PT teacher in the review of teaching;

3.10 access to professional development support and advice, and publications on teaching, from staff development;

3.11 invitation to school 'away days' and other open meetings to review and discuss teaching and course development within the school.

4   In addition, all PT teachers on contracts of 0.25 FTE and above should be entitled to:

4.1   access to the university's Certificate in Teaching in Higher Education;

4.2   a periodic individual review of teaching by an experienced teacher at the time of reappointment or renewal of PT contract, based on the university's staff development and appraisal scheme but emphasising only those aspects (usually teaching) relevant to the PT member of staff;

4.3   copies of course committee documentation and the right to attend course committee meetings and contribute to debate about teaching within the school.

5   PT teachers involved in marking should be provided with clear objectives and criteria for the assignments and questions they are marking and guidance on standards, including either examples of marked work or an opportunity to compare standards with an experienced teacher.

6   PT teachers allocated other teaching-related duties, such as personal tutoring, fieldwork supervision, undergraduate project supervision, postgraduate supervision, examinations or admissions, should be adequately briefed and trained for each additional type of duty and given access to a named advisor (usually the part-time teacher co-ordinator) for guidance and information;

7   How schools arrange to meet these entitlements should be documented in school reviews, which should comment on the adequacy of support and training for PT teachers and the effects of this on teaching quality within the school.

9.2   Supporting part-time teachers

Part-time teachers often feel that they are not fully included in the work of the department, although it is in everyone's interests that this should not be the case. It is particularly important that they should be involved in committees and working parties, both for the contribution they can make and for the sense of ownership this will generate for them. In a system where a great deal is implicit (such as what constitutes a 2:1) it is particularly helpful for part-time staff to take part in those discussions that help to provide reference points and examples.

Of course it is also vital to ensure that part-time staff are on circulation lists and email listings, so that they routinely receive the same information as full-time staff. There can be problems in communication when information is sent from the centre of a university, because the centre does not necessarily know about those staff whose employment is short, occasional and managed at departmental level. It then has to be the department's responsibility to make sure such information reaches all those who need it.

Another way of dealing with the sense of isolation that some part-time staff feel is to put them in touch with other part-time staff, perhaps by compiling a list of contact addresses or bringing all part-timers together for a social meeting that will encourage them to form their own network.

10 Staff development for research

In many institutions the main focus of staff development is on teaching, learning and assessment. It is easy to make the assumption that research, from the staff development point of view, will take care of itself, especially given its high priority in the system as a whole and the well-established mechanisms which support it both within and outside institutions. It is also normally the case that many research-oriented tasks, such as reviewing papers and grants, editing journals and organising conferences, have never been supported by any training provision whatsoever. Scholars learn these things by trial and error, and there is consequently considerable anxiety associated with many research-related activities. The lack of progress of some staff in their research may be partly due to the lack of staff development support in this area.

The development of research expertise, including issues to do with publication, is difficult to tackle at institutional level because, while there are some common issues that central programmes will deal with, much detailed information about research is subject-specific. Some staff will take an interest in staff development only if it deals with what they see as their central concern, which may well be research.

Some staff may have no significant publications record, and may feel pressured to publish. For them, sessions on writing for publication and on writing research proposals may be helpful. Many institutions organise sessions centrally on this topic, but there is usually value in a follow-up that will tackle issues from a more subject-specific perspective. A brainstorming session identifying possible topics for research may be useful. It may not have occurred to some that they might examine broader teaching, learning and assessment issues, or research their own practice and derive publications from it.

10.1 Information

Details of journals, their requirements and their status will be known about by individuals in departments, but it is quite possible that no one will ever have collected this information together for use by everyone. It is even less likely that journals dealing with teaching and learning issues in the discipline or in higher education in general will have been dealt with in this way. Sources of research funding is another vital area that is sometimes not well documented, even though the information is clearly vital in maximising the likelihood of success in researching.

10.2 Sharing expertise

Other staff may already have produced a substantial number of publications in journals, but look with envy at colleagues who seem to have broken through to another level. If they are to enhance their published output, in the form of books rather than journals, they may need to review their progress to date, to clarify their strengths and limitations, to find out how more established colleagues identify markets, deal with publishers, plan their research output to maximise their return and present themselves to their academic community. There may be a good deal of expertise within departments that is waiting to be tapped. An event that brings together established and aspiring authors of books or articles in the better refereed journals to share ideas may be very useful, as in the example over.

A RESEARCH DEVELOPMENT ACTIVITY

In the Faculty of Arts and Humanities at the University of Warwick, a number of staff who were established in journal publication wanted to know how they could emulate their colleagues who were succeeding in having books published.

An event was organised to bring the two groups together to share ideas. A two-hour session entitled 'Developing publications in Arts and Humanities' gave an opportunity for a panel of established authors to offer their experiences and advice, working through a list of topics that had been identified beforehand. These included:

- establishing and maintaining good relations with publishers

- finding an outlet for research that is not immediately marketable

- taking note of market requirements

- identifying gaps in existing markets

- presenting oneself as an author

- writing proposals / outlines

- managing work load

- knowing yourself, your capacities and limitations

- taking a cumulative approach to your work

- collaborating with colleagues.

A representative from publishing was also invited to provide another perspective.

10.3 Identifying areas of common interest

Staff do not necessarily read one another's publications or know in detail of their colleagues' research interests. A department may well be a collection of people who see themselves as having widely differing research interests. There may be some value in circulating details of current research interests, or of organising an event where staff can talk about their interests and any problems that currently confront them. Such sessions are frequently organised, of course, for postgraduate students, but they can be good for staff too. In this way, areas of common interest can be discovered, leading to the possibility of collaborative work.

10.4 Mounting departmental research conferences

Many departments host conferences periodically, and these can be a useful way of bringing the members of a department together in a common cause, as well as a means of exchanging information. There may be other departments in the institution working with a similar knowledge base and research methodology, where inter-departmental collaboration would be fruitful. Again, an event that brought people together to share interests might pay dividends.

Much research has to be tackled by teams of people, many of whom may be extremely individualistic. Indeed, their academic success to date may result in part from such individuality, and from an ability to work alone and unsupervised. Collaborative research requires an additional set of skills, to do with forming, developing and maintaining a team, sharing work, making meetings productive, and so on. These are skills we increasingly expect of students, but do not always ensure we develop among ourselves. The development of team working in a department can only really be done at departmental level. Whilst an external consultant can sometimes be useful here, this is exactly the kind of staff development that has to be owned and managed from within the department.

10.5 Staff development for research assistants and graduate teaching assistants

Many departments will have research assistants, and an increasing number will have graduate teaching assistants (GTAs). They will, of course, have their own research supervisors, but there may be value in organising meetings to discuss issues of common interest and to support staff development.

DEPARTMENT-SPECIFIC SUPPORT OF GTAS AT THE UNIVERSITY OF BRADFORD

A department-specific support programme for the development of graduate teaching assistants (GTAs) began at the University of Bradford in September 1994. Before this, support had generally been at an individual level and was usually provided by the tutor responsible for the particular teaching.

All departments were contacted by the newly appointed teaching quality adviser working within a recently established Teaching and Learning Development Unit. The type of support provided was dependent upon the amount of active participation which could be gained from the responsible tutors. Where this was fulsome, as in some cases, the lecturers had a clear view of the particular needs of their GTAs and it was possible to plan a full- or half-day event specifically for the department. Where the support was less active the teaching quality adviser would meet with members of the department to 'get a feel' for the kind of support needed, before planning the details of the provision in collaboration with the GTAs.

As their teaching role was not the prime activity of the postgraduates, each programme had to be short and context specific. It was also made explicit at the outset that the central aim of the programme was to improve the quality of the learning support and not to encourage GTAs to do more teaching.

The task of the GTAs at the first session was to use a generic plan to prioritise and contextualise the particular activities to be explored during the programme.

In the programmes facilitated by the teaching quality adviser, sessions, which were no longer than 1.5 hours, were spaced out, so that wherever possible, GTAs could link explorations of particular issues to their own practice. This iterative approach enabled the GTAs to bring the department's activities into each session and to challenge or confirm advice in the light of their own experience.

The sessions themselves were highly interactive and aimed to model active learning as well as provide a forum for reflection and debate. Although under considerable pressure to be highly productive researchers, the majority of GTAs were very enthusiastic towards the innovative ideas and this task-orientated approach. No programme lasted longer than 10 hours in total, and those concerned primarily with supporting laboratory demonstrators were considerable less.

It was obvious from this experience that there is much merit in a department-specific approach to GTA development; however, there are some drawbacks:

- GTAs are denied the opportunity of gaining from the experience of a wide range of peers.

- the particular language and cultural needs of international GTAs are less well supported.

- the approach is fairly time consuming for the central facilitator.

- group size is often rather small for the modelling of particular techniques.

In the second year of providing this support there has been a reduction of administration time on account of a raised awareness and a departmental expectation that this support should be made available to their GTAs.

The programme has also been valuable in providing a platform for the wider discussion of teaching and learning issues. Tutors involved in programme events have clearly welcomed the opportunity to examine their own practice and to challenge old assumptions. In some instances the ways in which the work of the responsible tutor and the GTA interrelate have been more clearly articulated.

POSTGRADUATE TRAINING IN THE THE DEPARTMENT OF PSYCHOLOGY
AT THE UNIVERSITY OF NOTTINGHAM

The module that we offer on teaching and communication skills has two purposes:

1 for reasons of teaching quality assurance, it is required training for any of our postgraduate students or research assistants who volunteer for paid teaching of undergraduates in our department.

2 as part of their generic training in research methods, and for career development purposes, it is required training for all our postgraduate research students (whether they teach or not). In particular, this is an area identified by ESRC as part of a broad postgraduate research training programme. It therefore forms part of fulfilling requirements for obtaining Mode A recognition for ESRC studentships.

The numbers of students taking the module in any one year are approx 12–15. The format consists of half-day interactive and practical workshops. The format may vary slightly depending on the particular topic, but normally includes role play or small-group problem-solving around case studies, etc. Total contact time for the whole module is approx. 18 hours.

The topics covered are:

• teaching in large groups: including practice and feedback in lecturing; preparation and use of visual aids; presentation style & delivery

• small-group teaching: including role play; case studies; ideas for promoting active learning; peer tutoring

• demonstrating in laboratory classes: including ideas for student projects; we also use peer tutoring here, with more experienced teaching assistants helping in small-group discussions

• assessment, feedback and evaluation: purpose of assessment; consideration of a variety of methods and their appropriateness; feedback to students; assessment of oral as well as written skills; evaluation of teaching.

At present we don't assess this module formally. However, those who teach on the module are asked to comment on students' progress and performance as part of the annual progress review for postgraduate students.

Finally, in addition to the above, we run other modules for postgraduates which cover oral and written presentation of research (e.g. conference papers and posters, journal articles), managing meetings effectively, dealing with the media, etc.

Claire O'Malley, Psychology, May 1996

10.6 Monitoring and reporting on sabbaticals and study leave

Study leave is the most popular (and expensive) form of staff development, and its benefits should be spread as widely as possible. It is useful to provide a means by which those who have had leave can feed back into the department a report on what they have been doing. It may be worth while holding an occasional meeting to discuss how people manage and get the most out of their study leave.

11 Evaluation of staff development activities

11.1 Evaluating the impact

If staff development is of value then it can, and should, be evaluated. The evaluation of staff development activities within institutions is often anecdotal and serendipitous.

It is important that evaluation takes place in order that

- the process of staff development can be improved;

- we enable ourselves to be accountable to all stakeholders;

- a case for more staff development can be made.

The evaluation of staff development activities should attempt to measure both the nature and the degree of change. Effective evaluation will depend on clear, defined and agreed parameters that are settled on before any activity takes place. There are several measurable areas of change that might result from training and development activities. These may include:

- behavioural: changes in patterns of behaviour

- functional: changes in practical operations

- attitudinal: changes in opinion or ways of thinking

- financial: the management of money and the direct effect on resources

- cognitive: knowledge and perception

- skill: expertise and practiced ability.

Kirkpatrick (1959) provides a four-level model for evaluation that is applicable to staff development. Each level of the model considers complementary aspects of development and training; they should not be regarded in any way as hierarchical.

REACTION This will establish what the participants felt about the activity; there is no focus on the learning that has taken place. Often measured by a questionnaire or a 'happy sheet'.

LEARNING This is concerned with internal validation where the focus is on the achievement of the stated objectives and the learning that has taken place. Information from this type of evaluation will assist in enhancing the quality of future activities.

BEHAVIOUR The focus is external validation and will look at the effective transfer of development and training activities to the 'work' environment. The emphasis is on the measurement of behavioural changes.

RESULTS This will establish how/if the activity has made a difference or impacted on the organisation.

If the levels are transferred into a set of basic questions, we might ask:

- did the participant enjoy the event?

- did the participant learn anything?

- was the learning transferred to the work situation?

- did the department and/or institution benefit?

In higher education the first two questions would normally be asked following a staff development activity. The latter two require responses at a different stage, as they cannot be answered immediately. For evaluation to be effective it should ideally be carried out in two stages – immediately after the activity and some time after.

EXAMPLE QUESTIONNAIRE

PART 1: BEFORE THE STAFF DEVELOPMENT ACTIVITY

Name................................... Department............................

1. Describe the proposed activity, including details of the dates, location and costs.
2. Indicate the departmental objectives the activity will help to achieve.
3. What skills and knowledge will be learnt as a result of this activity?
4. How will the skills and knowledge be applied in your work?
5. Senior colleague/ line manager's comment (including reference to targets and expectations)

Signature   Participant   date

Senior colleague/line manager   date

PART 2: IMMEDIATELY FOLLOWING THE STAFF DEVELOPMENT ACTIVITY

1. The best thing about the activity was . . .
2. The thing that could be changed in the future is . . .
3. The standard of delivery was   outstanding...............................poor
4. To what extend did the activity meet the agreed objectives (from part 1)?

                     Totally....................................not at all

5. How will the learning be applied?
6. What help or support will you need to put this into practice?
7. Agreed date to review

Signature   Participant   date

Senior colleague/line manager   date

PART 3: REVIEW TO MONITOR IMPACT OF STAFF DEVELOPMENT ACTIVITY

1. Has the learning been applied since the staff development activity?
2. To what extent have the agreed targets and objectives been met?
3. Have there been any additional benefits (improved quality of work, confidence, etc.)?
4. If learning has not been applied, please indicate the difficulties.
5. What further action is required?

Signature   Participant   date

Senior colleague/line manager   date

11.2 Links to future planning

Any evaluation activity should assist in providing information that will disseminate good practice and inform policy. Within departments there needs to be the structural mechanisms to ensure that this link is established and maintained. This is addressed in Chapter 5.

12 Useful publications and sources of expertise

1 Bibliography

Angelo, T. A. (1994) From Faculty Development to Academic Development. *American Association for Higher Education Bulletin*, June, pp. 2–7.

Blackwell, R. and McLean, M. (1996) Mentoring New University Teachers. *International Journal of Academic Development*, 1.2.

Brew, A. (ed.) (1995) *Directions in Staff Development. Buckingham*: Society for Research into Higher Education and Open University Press.

Candy, P. and Borthwick, J. (1994) The Ally Within: An Innovatory Approach to Networking and Staff Development. *Innovative Higher Education*, 18, 3, pp. 189–204.

DeZure, D. (1996) *Closer to the Disciplines*. American Association for Higher Education Bulletin, February, pp. 9–12.

Diamond, R. (1995) *The Disciplines Speak: Rewarding the Scholarly Professional, and Creative Work of Faculty*. Washington: American Association for Higher Education.

Gibbs, G. (1996) Supporting Educational Development within Departments. *International Journal of Academic Development*, pp. 27-27 1, 1.

Hounsell, D., McCulloch, M. and Scott, M (eds) (1996) *The ASSHE Inventory - Changing Assessment Practices in Higher Education*. Centre for Teaching and Learning, University of Edinburgh.

Hughes, P. and Thackwray, B. (1996) *The Staff Developer and Induction*. SEDA/UCoSDA Staff Development Paper No. 2.

Kirkpatrick, Donald L. (1994) *Evaluating training programmes: the four levels*. Berrett-Koehler, San Francisco.

Massey, W. F., Wilger, A. K. and Colbeck, C. (1994) Departmental Cultures and Teaching Quality: Overcoming 'Hallowed' Collegiality. *Change*, July/August, pp. 11–20.

Robertson, C. and Priest, J. (1995) *A Place of Learning – A Place for Learning*. Oxford: Oxford Brookes University.

Thackwray, B. (1997) *Effective Evaluation of Teaching and Development in Higher Education*. London Kogan Page.

Webb, G. (1996) *Understanding Staff Development*. Buckingham: Society for Research into Higher Education and Open University Press.

Wright, W. A. (ed.) (1995) *Teaching Improvement Practices: Successful Strategies for Higher Education*. Bolton, MA: Anker.

2   Web sites

ASSHE

http://www.tla.ed.ac.uk/asshepages/ASSHEhom.html

DeLiberations

An 'interactive magazine' on teaching and learning funded by the HEFCE.

http://www.lgu.ac.uk/deliberations/

Journal on Excellence in College Teaching

http://www.lib.muohio.edu/ject/

NCET National Council for Educational Technology

http://ncet.csv.warwick.ac.uk/

National Information Services and Systems

http://www.niss.ac.uk/

Netskills – training in electronic media

http://www.netskills.ac.uk/

Oxford Centre for Staff Development

30 publications, 200 workshops and short courses a year, and a network of 30 consultants

http://www.brookes.ac.uk/services/ocsd/

SEDA

TLTP Teaching and Learning Technology Programme

http://www.icbl.hw.ac.uk/tltp/

Universities and Colleges Staff Development Agency

Funded by subscription from universities and colleges

http://www.niss.ac.uk/education/ucosda.html

Universities and colleges sensitive map

http://scitsc.wlv.ac.uk/ukinfo/uk.map.html

Appendices

I   Staff development policy

Faculty of Technology, Kingston University

Foreword

This booklet brings together the public statements of this faculty's current staff development policy, as endorsed by the faculty board and faculty executive. This policy is presented in three parts:

Part I relates specifically to general management training and applies in various degrees to all staff of the faculty, be they technical, administrative, or academic.

Part II relates to teaching and learning and is of most relevance to the academic staff.

Part III relates to individual and group professional development, with a special section to each of the three groups of staff.

Funds are reserved within the faculty each year and are at the disposal of resource managers specifically to enable staff to engage in staff development activities. These notes clarify what activities are supported by the faculty. The university reserves additional funds for supporting staff development activities (e.g. Academic Efficiency Fund). It should not be presumed that such university and faculty funds are the only sources of 'staff development'. As part of the policy, staff are actively encouraged to seek opportunities for gaining additional support, particularly in association with sponsored research and consultancy activities.

J. J. Roberts, Dean
Faculty of Technology: April, 1994

PART I – MANAGEMENT TRAINING

All staff within the faculty require some aspect of 'management training'. Thus any schemes must be tailored to meet the particular requirements of the participants. The faculty is committed to promoting appropriate training in these areas, the major areas currently identified being:

1   management of time – applicable to all staff

2   people management and team building

3   course management

4   management of physical resources

  - material / stock control

  - financial aspects

  - machine usage, especially computing resources

5   marketing of skills

  - academic and technical

  (e.g. core courses, short courses, consultancy, research)

6   communications

  - all aspects: with colleagues, students, customers, etc.

7   personal development of management skills.

Some of these aspects are covered by courses already existing in the university, but aspects such as marketing, laboratory management, etc. could possibly be best covered by faculty schemes.

Approved by Faculty Board: 11th November 1992
Confirmed by Faculty Executive: 19th November 1992

PART II – TEACHING & LEARNING

The faculty wishes to promote the training of academic staff within the following key areas:

1 course design strategies for larger cohorts

2 assessment and maintenance of high course quality in the context of larger cohorts

3 facilitating effective student learning in large groups (lectures, etc.) and in small groups – e.g. laboratory work, seminars, tutorials

4 resource-efficient assessment of students

5 development of learning support materials – e.g. handouts, use of audio-visual aids, computer-based learning packages, etc.

6 improvement of student learning and skills, and the development of self-managed and peer-supported learning

7 provision of academic support for all students, including help for non-standard entry and those with special needs, etc.; promotion of equal opportunities.

Approved by Faculty Board, 11th November 1992
Confirmed by Faculty Executive, 19th November 1992

PART III – ACADEMIC STAFF

The faculty is committed to support all academic staff, both individually and in collaborative groups, in the maintenance and enhancement of their professional and academic subjectarea and teaching and learning expertise and of their awareness of current professional and industrial practice and needs. This supports university policy, for example, as represented in sections 7.2, 7.3 of the 1993 corporate plan. The major

mechanisms by which this support is provided are:

1 funding of attendance at internal and external training courses

2 funding of attendance at academic and professional conferences, symposia, colloquia and seminars

3 promotion of and financial support where possible for short visits and longer term secondments to UK and overseas universities

4 funding support for the mounting of academic and professional conferences, symposia, colloquia and seminars within the faculty

5 promotion of and financial support where possible for secondments to business and industrial organisations

6 dissemination of information about and promotion of participation in UK government- and European Community-funded schemes to promote collaboration between universities and industry

7 active encouragement of staff to undertake research, consultancy and other professional practice in their areas of expertise and teaching and learning.

The head of school has the responsibility for ensuring that all staff have access to information about and support for staff development and, via the appraisal mechanism, for ensuring that appropriate development, within resources limitations, is undertaken by all staff in the school.

Approved by Faculty Executive, 10th February 1994
Approved by Faculty Board, 24th February 1994

PART III – ADMINISTRATIVE STAFF

The faculty is committed to support all administrative staff in the pursuance of their duties. These duties include the exercise and development of administrative, managerial and personal expertise to provide the appropriate administrative services for teaching, research and consultancy. This supports university policy, for example, as represented in section 7.2 of the 1993 corporate plan.

The staff development supported at line-management level includes:

1 funding of attendance at internal and external training courses

2 funding of attendance at exhibitions, conferences, symposia, colloquia and seminars

3 support for part-time academic studies allowing staff to attain higher professional qualifications

4 encouragement of staff to widen their knowledge base by involvement in the university administrators' networking scheme

5 encouragement of staff to undertake/collaborate in research and consultancy which is relevant to the development of their administrative expertise.

The faculty admin manager and admin officers have a responsibility, through the appraisal scheme, to ensure all administrative staff have access to information about, and support for, a wide range of staff development opportunities and for ensuring that appropriate development, within resource limitations, is undertaken by all administrative staff.

Amended and approved by Faculty Board, 24th February 1994

Approved by Faculty Executive, 17th March 199

PART IV – TECHNICAL STAFF

The faculty is committed to support all technical staff in the pursuance of their duties. These duties include the exercise and development of technical, managerial and personal expertise to provide the appropriate professional services for teaching, research and consultancy. This supports university policy, for example as presented in section 7.2 of the 1993 corporate plan.

The staff development supported at line-management level includes:

1 funding of attendance at internal and external training courses

2 funding of attendance at exhibitions, conferences, symposia, colloquia and seminars

3 support for part-time academic studies allowing staff to attain higher professional qualifications

4 encouragement of staff to widen their knowledge base by involvement in the university administrators' networking scheme

5 encouragement of staff to undertake/collaborate in research and consultancy which is relevant to the development of their administrative expertise.

The faculty technical manager and technical officers have a responsibility, through the appraisal scheme, to ensure all technical staff have access to information about, and support for, a wide range of staff development opportunities and for ensuring that appropriate development, within resource limitations, is undertaken by all technical support staff.

Approved by Faculty Executive, 10th February 1994

Approved by Faculty Board, 24th February 1994

II   Staff development policy

Faculty of Humanities, Bath College of Higher Education

1   Background:

One of the responsibilities of faculty board is to advise the dean on staff development activities. This paper was requested by faculty board at its last meeting (7.12.94) in order to facilitate the prioritisation and support of staff development within the faculty of humanities.

2   Aims of faculty staff development policy

2.1   To use the college staff appraisal scheme to identify individuals' development needs, and to respond to them as appropriate.

2.2   To prioritise such individual requirements within the context of the faculty development plan and the college's strategic plan.

2.3   To identify individual members of staff whose effectiveness could be improved by the provision of a programme of staff development.

2.4   To provide mechanisms by which the professional aspirations of individual members of staff can be met within the context of faculty requirements.

2.5   To generate staff development activities from within the faculty, pooling expertise and encouraging members of the faculty to support each other in the acquisitions of new skills.

2.6   To provide a flow of information, through faculty and school boards, about courses, conferences, workshops, etc., which might meet the development needs of individuals and groups of staff.

2.7   To provide induction into the faculty's activities for new members of staff.

2.8   To provide resources, within budgetary constraints, for the support of prioritised staff development within the faculty.

2.9   To monitor faculty expenditure on staff development and to ensure value for money in whatever activities the faculty supports.

2.10   To provide input into the college's strategic plan for staff development and to liaise with appropriate college personnel and developments in this area.

2.11   To ensure that faculty staff are aware of both faculty and college policy on staff development.

2.12   To ensure that the college's equal opportunities policy is implemented at all levels of faculty activity in the area of staff development.

2.13   To co-operate wherever possible with other faculties in the provision of staff development.

2.14   To support members of staff as providers of staff development to other institutions.

3   Examples of staff development

3.1   Attendance at conferences of short courses enabling staff to acquire or update specific skills, as in information technology, curriculum design and development, administration, health and safety.

3.2   Attendance at courses or conferences which enable members of staff to develop pedagogical skills and to meet new pedagogical tasks, such as the supervision of research students.

3.3   Exchanges with members of staff in institutions at home and abroad, bringing the opportunity to strengthen external contacts and to acquire new and challenging working experience.

3.4   Timetable relief for members of staff engaged in activities specifically identified as central to the faculty development plan, such as curriculum development and design.

3.5   'Cascade-effect' seminars led by individuals who have attended seminars or courses which might be of direct use to groups of staff in the faculty.

3.6   In-house programmes of staff development generated by current expertise within the faculty, as in desktop publishing or the design and implementation of student evaluation exercises.

Neil Sammells, March 1995

Institutional policy for staff development

III   University of Anon City (Open University)

Introduction

This statement has been formulated by the college's staff development committee and approved by the academic board. It applies to all members of the full-time teaching and non-teaching staff and is based on the assumption that an effective policy for staff development will help:

(a) to ensure that the best possible learning opportunities are available;

(b) to enable the college and its staff to respond effectively to changing circumstances;

(c) to enhance the personal and professional satisfaction of staff.

Responsibility for staff development

Overall responsibility for the implementation of staff development policy rests with the staff development committee, faculty committees, and individual departments within the college. Procedures for initiating and gaining approval for specific activities are as outlined below. A member of the full-time teaching staff acts as staff development co-ordinator for the college and is attached to the Educational Services Unit. He or she is responsible for matters such as collecting and disseminating information relating to staff development, providing a counselling service for staff, organizing in-service induction courses, liaising with departments about the implementation of staff development policy, and preparing a staff development handbook.

The aims of staff development

Staff development is an integral part of the life of the college, continuing throughout the entire career of a member of the staff and aiming to harmonize the needs of the individual with the needs of the institution. Within this general framework, the academic board will endeavour to implement a policy that:

(a) enables staff to extend their knowledge and skills and to operate as effectively as possible in their current roles;

(b) allows staff to review their needs and requirements and to suggest ways of meeting these;

(c) provides opportunities for staff to prepare themselves for changing duties and responsibilities within the college;

(d) services to increase job satisfaction and to facilitate career progression.

It is recognised that the emphasis given to these various aims will differ from one member of staff to another, depending partly on the individual's experience and aspirations.

Identification of staff development needs

Staff development needs and requirements will become apparent in a number of ways. Some will arise from self-appraisal, informal discussions with colleagues, or the deliberations of course committees. Others will be identified more formally, perhaps as part of procedures leading up to the preparation of the college's academic development plan.

All members of staff are invited to review regularly their development needs and identify priorities. Everyone should have a job description, specifying his or her duties and responsibilities. Heads of department are asked to arrange annual development discussions with individual members of staff, and to use these discussions as a basis for drawing up plans for the department as a whole.

Faculty committees are required to consider staff development needs and activities relevant to the work of the departments within the faculty. They report to the staff development committee each year at its final meeting in the summer term. The chief administrative officer and heads of the academic support services (Computer Centre, Educational Services Unit, and Library) are also required to submit reports to the committee.

Staff development activities

Participation in staff development activities is normally regarded as voluntary, except in the case of attendance at induction courses for new untrained members of staff, which is compulsory. The college is keen to encourage the widest possible range of staff development activities and, in order to promote this, provides a special budget allowance to be allocated by the staff development committee. In addition, there are various staff development initiatives that may not require resource provision (e.g. planned changes in responsibility, committee membership, formation of special interest-groups), and all departments are urged to exploit these possibilities as much as possible.

External courses and conferences:

Applications to attend external courses and conferences require the head of department's support. In addition, the following requirements apply.

(a)   short courses (less than four weeks' duration) and conferences: approval is required in advance from the chair of the staff development committee (fees and expenses are normally refunded in full; total annual expenditure is reported to the governing body);

(b)   part-time courses (normally by day release) leading to recognized qualifications: approval for study leave is required in advance from the chair of the staff development committee (fees and expenses are normally refunded in full or in part by the LEA);

(c)   full-time courses leading to recognized qualifications: applications for secondment are considered by the LEA, following a recommendation from the academic board and the staff development committee.

Staff who are studying part-time may apply to the governing body for paid leave of absence to revise for examinations (15 days maximum).

Sabbatical leave :

A limited number of staff may be granted up to a year's sabbatical leave to undertake a specific assignment in association with an outside body or organization. Assignments that strengthen links between the college and industry, commerce, and professional bodies are especially encouraged.

Applications for sabbatical leave from members of staff with at least five years' service are considered by the LEA, following a recommendation from the academic board and the staff development committee.

Internal courses and related activities:

Staff are encouraged to take advantage of development opportunities already available within the college's approved programme of courses. The staff development committee is responsible each year for arranging a special programme of in-house seminars and short courses.

The staff development committee also organizes a ten-day induction course for new staff during the autumn term. This is compulsory for all new untrained staff with less than three years' full-time teaching experience, and staff are eligible for a reduction in their class-contact time.

Departments are required to provide each new member of staff with an appropriate 'mentor' to act as a source of advice and support.

Special projects:

In addition to the activities identified above, the staff development committee invites applications for support for individual projects designed to meet specified staff development needs, e.g. research and consultancy, study visits, course evaluation projects, and short attachments to an outside firm. Limited financial support is available from the staff development budget, and

members of staff can apply for timetable remission from class-contact time (this will not normally exceed four hours per week).

This illustration of a typical policy statement is retitled but taken from:

Open University Book 5 Managing Staff, E324 Education: A Third-Level Course Management in Post – Compulsory Education. Part 4: Institutional Policies for Staff Development section 2.4 pp. 105–107 Open University, 1984. ISBN 0335 132561

IV Staff and learning development policy

LSU, College of Higher Education

1 Background

The policy is developed in response to the finds of an inspection during 1995/1996. It is aimed at providing training and support for all members of staff within the Faculty of Education (full- and part-time), for teaching practice supervisors, mentors and all associated staff involved in the delivery and planning of courses. The policy was produced by the chair of the learning development committee (LDC) in conjunction with the dean of faculty and members of the LDC.

2 Responsibilities

The LDC reports to the faculty and on a management by exception basis the LSU Learning Resources Committee (LRC). It has the responsibility of achieving the following goals:

a)   establishing staff development priorities based on evidence from inspection reports, external examiners and on an analysis of changing requirements of courses;

b)   meeting the relevant targets outlined in the

faculty development plan;

c)   managing the staff development budget;

d)   auditing teaching and assessment methods and the use of learning resources within the faculty and making proposals for developments;

e)   liaising with the CQAC, the partnership and research faculty committees in order to identify new aspects of development and monitor progress;

f)   to establish a database of expertise within the faculty and to identify and encourage ways in which this can be used to the benefit of faculty members;

g)   to record the progress of development events/activities and report progress to the appropriate college committees.

3   Mechanisms

a)   Strategic planning

Planning of staff development activities will involve consultation with the dean and other committees, primarily the partnership group and the course quality assurance committee (CQAC) and will relate directly to achieving the faculty and LDC strategic goals.

b)   Decision making

The dean and the LDC will control the budget and will allocate funds (in the short term) according to the contribution an activity will have in achieving the strategic goals. The achievement of longer term priorities will also be considered on the basis of priority.

c)   Identification of staff development needs

Short-term strategic goals are stated in the faculty development plan. Longer term goals will be identified by the LDC through the teaching and

assessment audit, data from course evaluations, appraisals, discussions at faculty meetings and other appropriate sources.

d)   Sharing of expertise

The LDC will identify and implement strategies that enable staff to learn from peers by having access to each other's expertise.

e)   Access to information on learning and teaching developments

f)   Evaluation of staff development activities and effectiveness

The LDC will evaluate and monitor the effectiveness (in terms of changes in behaviour) of all activities. This will be reported to LDC meetings and used to inform future planning.

g)   Links between the LDC and LSU central committees

The LDC will have representation on the LRC. The chair and one other member will attend the LRC. It is essential to maintain links with the central committee decisions and college-wide policy. Following meetings of the respective committees, reports will be made to the LDC.

4   Staff development priorities

4.1   Short-term priorities are to assist the work of the faculty in achieving a successful OFSTED reinspection and are incorporated in the faculty development plan. They include:

a)   establishing a mechanism of training tutors, supervisors, school mentors and classroom supervisors of the final year students. This will be achieved by a series of training days. Training will begin with staff during October reading week. For those involved in the BEd final teaching practice, training will be in January, and for

- formal inclusion of the HERDSA checklist on valuing teaching (and the subsequent HERDSA document for individual teachers, Challenging Conceptions of Teaching: Some Prompts for Good Practice – December 1992)

- implementation of desired teaching quality programme, including annual teaching effectiveness measurement by all staff by student and/or peer review

- teaching effectiveness viewed from a developmental perspective, encouragement of teaching portfolios and progress linked to personal joint goal setting and review

- operation of a faculty database on the measurement and audit of teaching and the maintenance of a teaching resource centre

- teaching development advisers

- leadership, management and co-ordination of teaching development activities, including a newly created tenurable associate professor position in 1993

- increased support for teaching innovation and research under PDP schemes and faulty semesters to investigate alternative and innovative teaching strategies.

Professional involvement to include part-time teaching, supervision of project work and participation in clinical teaching schemes to be increased from 10 per cent to 20 per cent over five years. Human resource development to include induction courses for new staff; teaching workshops; adoption of detailed faculty policy on teaching criteria for tenure and promotion; active adjunct professor scheme; final-year honours students as teaching assistants; dean's awards for excellence and innovation; encouragement and support for existing teaching interest group, appointment of associate professor 1993 to co-ordinate.

Teaching and learning process in the next decade

A number of broad contextual issues will have a significant impact upon change in the learning environment in the law and justice studies areas.

The move to quality

At national, institutional and faculty levels there is a move to address the issue of quality. At one level it is likely that this will manifest itself in the development of mechanistic definitions and criteria of measurement, perhaps in the form of quantified performance indicators to which incentives and disincentives (including financial) will be attached. Fortunately a more enlightened level of thought will prevail which seeks to evaluate quality through more informed judgement and encourage and support a framework to undertake improvement. The path of continual improvement will be sustained only by a willingness on the part of the learning community to recognise the need for change for improvement and to have the motivation to undertake concrete things to improve rather than meet predetermined outcome targets.

The legitimate stakeholders

Over the next ten years there will be a working out in practice of the changing roles of the various stakeholders in tertiary learning institutions, including the Faculty of Law. This will result in different sharing arrangements. There will be a change from teaching to learning and to the recognition of a more significant and responsible role for the students in the learning process and greater responsiveness by teachers to students and the proper role and place. A climate of mutual respect, trust and open communication will be enhanced. It is probable that, whilst the views of employers and professional groups remain influential and of continued significance, the level of intrusive prescription will come to be viewed as less legitimate as a national or perhaps international perspective is taken. National mutual recognition legislation to be introduced into federal and state parliaments will seek that national approach at the level of vocational qualifications and subsume localised differences within a wider perspective.

The meaning of and means to quality

Over the next ten years debate and activity will take place, initially in attempting to define or determine what quality is and subsequently to identify the means of achieving or at least improving towards quality. Large portions of this activity will be sterile in terms of wasted energies seeking to define and quantify. Throughout the decade, substantial improvements will occur through the process of evaluation, research, consultation and action.

More active consideration of teaching and learning

Over the next decade the framework will provide renewed focus on this activity of universities, and more so in particular universities such as QUT. This will be driven in part by renewed federal government interest in quality in higher education and the provision of competitive funding. There is likely to be some tension in the working out of different priorities in respect of teaching and learning priorities relative to other legitimate activities such as research. At individual and faculty levels there will be greater experimentation and innovation, including greater emphasis on self-learning, more interactive learning environments and more flexible learning modes. There will be increasing reliance on technology in support of the greater flexibility and its more effective outcomes relative to delivery by teaching in lecture format. There will

be greater attention to design of units by individual teachers and teams to ensure more coherent fit of formal requirements, content, teaching methods, assessment and resources.

Resources and processes

Existing teaching and learning strategies rely heavily upon processes developed over time to support them. These processes range from institutional administration and support services to documented policies and procedures, to capital and human and other resource disposition. The tradition to date has relied heavily on teaching through delivery of content by lecture. The changes which will occur will be impeded significantly unless new processes and resource distributions are developed in support of substantive changes in learning strategies. Management of the change in terms of the organisational structures and processes will be as important to success as the progress towards identifying and implementing the changes themselves.

VI A strategic plan to improve teaching and reward teaching excellence

Division of Professional Practice, University of Cincinnati

(excerpts from the mission statement of the Division of Professional Practice)

The co-operative system of education, founded at the University of Cincinnati in 1906, seeks to enhance learning through the integration of theory and practice by an alternation of classroom study with paid discipline- and career-related work experiences. The Division of Professional Practice is the programme's management unit for the colleges on the Clifton campus. The faculty of the division have the responsibility to develop and co-ordinate the student work experiences, as to content, direction and quality. This role also involves preparing students for effective programme participation, assessment of student performance, awarding of credit for work terms, co-ordination of student participation arrangements with the colleges and certifying student completion of the co-operative component of degree requirements. The unit's primary goal in providing the co-operative courses (co-ordinated, monitored and graded discipline-related work experiences) for participating academic units is to develop competencies that are deemed important by faculty in the disciplines and by professional practitioners. Through critical appraisals by work supervisors, counselling and individualised instruction by professional practice faculty, students are given a realistic test of career interests and aptitudes, gain understanding about the realities of the world of work and learn many other things about people, practices and technology that can best be learned in a real-time work environment. Through multiple individual sessions with students, reviews of work reports and various quality control mechanisms, the division guides and evaluates student learning from co-op, rather than assume that it naturally takes place as a matter of course.

Project to improve and reward teaching

As a participant in the university-wide project to improve and reward teaching, the faculty of the Division of Professional Practice has approved, as our PIRT project, a five-year educational strategic plan.

Mission of the educational strategic plan

The mission of the division's educational strategic plan is to develop and implement, over the next five years, a strategy which will encourage an increased unit focus on maximising student learning from participation in the co-operative education programme. Recognition for the priority of the plan will be reflected through consideration in budget allocations, faculty reward systems and workload design.

Goals of the educational strategic plan

1 To identify the fundamental instructional goals of the professional practice educational strategic plan.

2 To develop a model syllabus including expectations for the professional practice instruction, which will optimise student learning.

3 To develop a model syllabus including expectations for the division's professional development I course, which will ensure that students are prepared for effective participation in the professional practice programme.

4 To develop and/or revise the appropriate instructional tools or methods to support the division's mission of professional practice instruction.

5 To develop instruments or methods of assessment to determine overall effectiveness in meeting the fundamental instructional goals of the professional practice educational strategic plan.

6 To develop appropriate faculty reward systems for performance that meets or exceeds expectations.

Educational strategic plan (sample goals, objectives and action steps)

Goal 1: To identify the fundamental instructional goals of the professional practice educational strategic plan

Objectives

1   Determine the relevant educational outcomes from participation in the professional practice programme.

2   Assess the relative importance of each.

3   Categorise these outcomes into comparable groups.

4   Determine the fundamental instructional goals.

Action steps

1   Form an ad hoc committee of the PIRT steering committee to analyse the educational outcomes of the professional practice programme.

2   The committee will solicit faculty input as needed.

3   The committee will analyse this input as well as other relevant information as they determine the fundamental instructional goals of the educational strategic plan.

4   The ad hoc committee will report their finding to the PIRT steering committee for clarification, revision and/or approval.

5   The PIRT steering committee will present recommendations to the professional practice faculty as to these fundamental instructional goals and lead the faculty towards agreement on these goals.

Goal 6: To develop appropriate faculty reward systems for performance that meets or exceeds expectations

Objectives

1   To develop a forum wherein each faculty member is given the opportunity to share current syllabi, methods and tools of teaching, to present outside learning from conferences and seminars, and to share any other developmental information with the faculty at large.

2   To create an annual event which recognises achievements by faculty in the division of professional practice.

Action steps

1   Utilise faculty meeting, 1/2 day workshops or periodic retreats as a vehicle for the sharing of information among professional practice faculty.

2   Form a committee on faculty rewards and recognition to develop an annual faculty appreciation event.

VII   Guidance on mentoring
University of Durham, Personnel Handbook, 3.8

These guidelines are intended to assist departments introducing the practice of mentoring, individual members of staff who are taking on the role of mentor, and new members of staff, who should also be provided with this guidance. The guidance, which has been drawn up using comments from members of staff with experience on both sides of the mentoring process, combines what is considered to be best practice outside the university with a regard for the particular circumstances of work within it.

Mentors should also make themselves familiar with the university's policies and procedures concerning probation and promotion, details of which are available in the 'Personnel Handbook' in information centres. Training workshops on mentoring are open to all members of staff. Further advice is available from the staff development and training adviser.

Chairmen/women of boards of studies and of schools should note that it has been agreed as a matter of staffing policy that all probationary teaching staff must be provided with a mentor on appointment.

Section 1: General Guidance

Mentoring is an informal and supportive relationship whereby a more experienced member of staff undertakes to help a new member of staff learn his/her job and its context in the university.

A mentor is:

- preferably, someone who broadly shares a new member of staff's professional or technical expertise;

- nominated by the appropriate head of section from staff not on probation.

A mentor is not:

- a substitute for effective line management, and therefore should not be the line manager or supervisor;

- the head of section;

- preferably, a new member of staff's appraiser.

A mentor can provide:

- initial departmental induction;

- observation and hands-on experience of work tasks;

- instruction in work processes;

- examples of, and guidance on, acceptable standards of work;

- information, advice and guidance on departmental, faculty, university and college procedures;

- guidance on departmental culture – 'the way we do things here'.

A mentor should be prepared to:

- initiate regular meetings with a new member of staff and be available, within reason, on request;

- assist with any problems relating to the performance of duties which a new member of staff chooses to raise;

- appreciate a new member of staff's differing experience and needs;

- accept that a new member of staff will wish to seek advice and support from a variety of colleagues;

- respect the importance of trust in the mentoring relationship.

A mentor should be able to:

- listen actively and attentively;

- ask open and appropriate questions;

- reflect back feelings and opinions he/she observes;

- make suggestions without sounding prescriptive;

- summarise the main points of discussions;

- give constructive, positive and precise feedback.

Section 2: Academic staff

For academic staff, a mentor can:

- provide basic information such as an outline of the year's programme of teaching and research activities, including deadlines, e.g. for examination questions, pressure on laboratory space, meetings and times for submission of items, registering and upgrading research students;

- help in preparing and structuring lectures;

- allow a new member of staff to observe their lectures, seminars, tutorials and research supervision;

- attend a new member of staff's lectures and provide constructive feedback;

- share lectures and seminars with a new member of staff;

- discuss the construction of examination questions;

- advise on or explain departmental marking conventions;

- offer feedback on the writing of research articles and conference papers;

- suggest appropriate vehicles for publications;

- help to prepare research submissions and other reports;

- offer advice on relevant administrative duties;

- help and advise, in due course, with interviewing potential students.

For probationary lecturers, a mentor should:

- be familiar with the university's guidance on probation and promotion;

- expect to be consulted by the chairman or chairwoman of the board of studies when asked to report formally on progress.

The academic staffing committee (promotion and probation) believes it is helpful if mentors provide a written report to the chairman or chairwoman of the board of studies, which can then be forwarded in support of the recommendation made.

VIII Academic mentors – code of practice
University of Hull

1 The academic mentor

The department will appoint an academic mentor to every probationary member of staff, who should be informed of this before teaching duties begin. The mentor's duties will commence with the signing of the contract and continue to the end of the formal period of probation.

2 Appointment of the mentor

The appointment will be made by the head of department and notified to the director of personnel and to the teaching and learning in higher education programme tutor. The mentor will be an experienced colleague sympathetic to the probationer's field of teaching and research. In small departments this responsibility may regularly fall to the same member of staff, but otherwise what could be a heavy, if temporary, burden should be distributed as widely as possible. The head of department should not normally fulfil this role, as it will be in the probationer's interest to have a source of advice independent from the head, who will have to make the recommendation to confirm probation. In the case of a breakdown of relations between mentor and probationer, the head may need to change the mentor, but will retain the final responsibility of appointment. The probationer can appeal to the dean if it is felt that the head of department is not acting reasonably in selecting the mentor.

3   General responsibilities

The work of the mentor must be tailored to the particular needs of the probationer and department. Although by definition no probationer is a fully fledged teacher and researcher, most will have experience in both fields, and this must be assessed and respected. Three general areas of advice and guidance can be identified.

a)   Departmental and university culture

General induction into how the system works in theory and practice, and how the probationer may relate to changes in progress. The effectiveness of this process will be conditioned by the availability of adequate documentation on central and departmental practice (including this code of practice). Here, as in other aspects, the mentor will in part act as a point of referral, recommending whom to approach in the department or elsewhere in the university for specialist information.

b)   Teaching

Mentors will advise probationary members of staff on aspects of teaching methods and programmes as necessary. Selection committees will decide which probationers will be required to attend the university's teaching and learning in higher education programme. The mentor is an essential part of the programme: ensuring attendance (and the time to attend) and discussing teaching methods, teaching materials, assessment, the design of courses, and the compiling of a teaching portfolio, which is a requirement of the programme. The mentors will observe these probationers' teaching and give feedback. Mentors of probationers who wish to undertake the university's certificate of initial teaching competence will submit a report, as part requirement for assessment, which will be based on evidence from regular discussion, observation of teaching and supervision of other aspects of teaching, including marking students' work.

c)   Research

Mentors should give advice on publications and grant applications, and comment on drafts of both of these. They should also advise on research targets and on how to balance the demands of teaching, research and administration, and, where necessary, protect the probationer's research time from other pressures.

4   Staff training

The mentor will monitor the probationer's participation in training courses, advising on additional training and discussing progress. When specific and potentially significant advice is given by a mentor (for example, to attend a relevant course) a note confirming the advice should be sent to the probationer/temporary lecturer and a copy kept by the mentor.

5   Mentor, head of department and appraisal

The relationship between the mentor and the probationer will be continuous and largely informal, although the mentor should arrange an initial meeting soon after the probationer arrives. The mentor can act as a channel of communication between the head of department and the probationer, but must not displace the head's responsibilities for managing the teaching and research of all members of the department. The mentor/probationer relationship is separate from the formal and confidential system of appraisal, but to avoid the creation of too confusing a structure of advice, and as long as appraisal remains formative, the appraiser will normally be either the mentor or the head of department.

6 Assistance to mentor

A short training course will be made available for mentors as part of the staff development programme.

7 Non-probationary new staff

Fixed-term temporary lecturers should be treated in all respects like lecturers on probation. Many of the needs outlined above will be shared by those appointed to permanent posts without a probationary period. In these cases heads of department should use their discretion to implement any part of this system as appropriate.

8 Graduate teaching assistants

(there is a separate document: GTAs: Guidelines for Heads of Departments)

GTAs are expected to teach up to six hours a week – no more than 72 hours a semester – with relatively modest amounts of preparation and supervised assessment. Only in exceptional circumstances should the GTA's teaching be with or for the research supervisor. GTAs will be required to attend part or all of the teaching and learning in higher education introductory programme, depending on the nature of their teaching duties. As in the case of probationers and temporary lecturers, mentors should allow adequate time to attend, observe teaching and discuss progress, and also ensure that teaching loads are not excessive.

IX   Peer report: teaching evaluation

City University of Hong Kong

Comments by:

On aspects of the teaching of:

Directions

Listed below are some significant aspects of the teaching role. They are provided to help you think systematically about your colleague's performance in these areas. Please comment on each of the categories based on your examination of the relevant sources of evidence at your disposal. If you feel that you are unable to respond to a particular item please comment to that effect at the appropriate place and indicate why. Your role in the evaluation of your colleague's teaching is important. Please complete your comments carefully.

1. Subject expertise

Refers to your colleague's 'expertness' within the particular discipline. You should consider grasp of the discipline; critical evaluation of new positions, theories and research findings, efforts in maintaining up-to-dateness; and ability to apply the results of research and theory to the development of their modules.

Comment:

Source of evidence:

2. Module presentation

Refers to your colleague's ability to design an academic course of appropriate levels. You should consider issues such as the suitability and currency of reference materials; consistency between objectives, content, processes, and planned assessment; and innovations introduced to the module.

Comment:

Source of evidence:

3. Promotion of student learning

Refers to your colleague's ability to encourage deep approaches to learning on the part of students. You should consider issues such as the quality of student handouts; appropriateness of strategies used to achieve module objectives; appropriateness of assessment programmes; the provision of feedback; and the quality and nature of media support materials.

Comment:

Source of evidence:

4. Module organisation

Refers to your colleague's ability to plan for and manage the human and material resources necessary to support an academic programme effectively. You should consider issues such as the availability of reading materials in the library; preparation of guidelines for supporting staff; supervision of supporting staff; and arrangements for special facilities.

Comment:

Source of evidence:

5. The support of institutional teaching goals

Refers to your colleague's willingness to support and competence in supporting both the institution's and the department's teaching missions. Your should consider issues such as submission of required documentation; contribution to course planning teams; and contribution to the enhancement of teaching in general.

Comment:

Source of evidence:

6. Supervision

Refers to your colleague's ability to encourage and guide students towards the successful completion of projects. You should consider issues such as awareness of a range of appropriate methodologies; ability to produce clear criticisms for students on their reports; and ability to identify vocational concerns in the marketplace.

Comment:

Source of evidence:

7. General comments

In this category you should note any other points of which you are aware and which you consider are relevant to your colleague's teaching.

Comment:

Source of evidence:

Signature of peer:

Comments of staff under review:

Signature of reviewer:

X   Peer review of teaching

University of Loughborough Quality Assessment Unit

Guidelines on observation of teaching

Introduction

These notes are intended to provide advice and ideas for staff undertaking observation of teaching – both those observing and those being observed. They are intended to cover general principles that will be applicable to both formal and informal assessments.

The notes are not intended to be prescriptive, as the process of observation is most effective when it has been developed between those involved.

Reasons for observing teaching

The main aim is to help staff, particularly in a time of rapid change, to reflect critically upon their teaching through planned and systematic observation and mutual analysis. Feedback from observation frequently stimulates staff to try out new ideas, reaffirms what is effective in existing practice and helps modify current techniques. All these processes help to improve the quality of student learning.

Overview of the suggested procedures

Preparation for observing a colleague's teaching is fairly straightforward and normally involves:

- agreeing who is going to observe the session;

- deciding upon the session to be observed;

- deciding upon the observation process;

- undertaking the observation;

- the observed and observer discussing the session;

- the observed and observer discussing the

outcomes to be recorded;

- the observed identifying activities and strategies for improvement of performance;

- the observed collating the records of observation and subsequent development programme in their teaching portfolio.

Before the observation

Selecting the observer

It is desirable that the observer is known to, and respected by, the person being observed. There should be a professional and trusting relationship between the two for the observation process to provide maximum benefit to both.

Deciding upon what session to observe

It is best to decide which session is to be observed through discussion between the observed and the observer. Aim for no more than one hour of observation. This could be a complete lecture, or part of a practical session (say the first and last 30 minutes).

Deciding upon what is to be done during the observation

Observed and observer should spend some time before the session discussing the process, e.g.:

- where the observer should sit, or whether it is appropriate to wander around (in practical sessions it may be valuable to talk with or observe the students);

- when observed and observer will meet to discuss the session; this is best done within a short time of the observed session (ideally immediately after, but otherwise as soon as possible), as it is easier to recall detail immediately.

During the observation

The process

There are four stages in the teaching process which can be identified in any lecture, seminar, tutorial, fieldwork or laboratory session:

- planning before the session;
- the introduction of the session;
- the delivery and implementation of the prepared plans;
- the conclusion of the session.

Question for the observation

The observer and observed should have a number of aspects and questions in mind when discussing and designing the process of observation. These could include:

planning the session:

- how does the plan relate to previous sessions?
- are there clear aims and objectives?
- how does the session fit in with the overall programme for the module?
- are resources (AVA, handouts, tasks) available at the appropriate points?

introducing the session to the students:

- is it clear to the students how this session relates to previous work?
- does the introduction 'set the scene' for the session, giving students a clear overview of the way it will develop?

delivering and developing the plans:

- is the communication of ideas relevant, clear and coherent?
- is there opportunity for the students to clarify their understanding? How is this handled?
- what strategies are used to gain attention, to

refocus at intervals and to ensure attention is maintained?

- are the students motivated?
- are the teaching methods appropriate to the tasks in hand?
- are there opportunities for the students to think, question and feed back?
- what modes of delivery are used; is more than one mode used?

concluding the session:

- is the session drawn to a satisfactory conclusion (or an ongoing series of conclusions)?
- is there a summary of the main ideas or a review of the point reached so far?
- does the conclusion look forward to the next session?

After the observation

The purpose of discussion and analysis after the observation is to provide an informed and reliable view of the session which allows the observed to gain from an independent perspective. Observed colleagues may wish to initiate a discussion beginning with their own self-assessment of the observed session or they may prefer the initial comments to come from the assessor. Either way it is easier to recall detail if the discussion follows as soon as possible after the observed session. Points for discussion will arise naturally from the assessor's report and from the list of effective teaching behaviours.

The ground rules for worthwhile discussion include:

- being a good listener;
- asking helpful questions;
- giving and receiving feedback;
- helping to develop an action plan.

XI	Peer observation report form
	University of Southampton

Observation note (for use in observed teaching and learning sessions)

(Based on HEFCE assessors' form)

Name ....

Subject .... Module / course title ....

Assessor .... Length of session .... hrs   Length of observation .... hrs

Number of students present .... Composition of the group ....

Level / year of study .... Mode of study: FT PT Other ....

Type of activity: Lecture Seminar Workshop Practical Tutorial Other

Which of the learning objectives of the course / module are relevant to this teaching / learning session?

....

Teaching: Please comment on the effectiveness of each of the following elements and the extent to
which the objectives planned are achieved

Comment on the effectiveness of this element of the session

Planning

Content

Methods

Pace

Use of examples

Overall comments:

Student participation: to what extent was student participation intended and how far did it occur as planned; what evidence was there of student engagement with the session; what evidence of the learning objectives being achieved?

Accommodation and resources: how effective was the use of the room and layout, specialist equipment and material, visual aids, IT, etc.?

Overall quality of the session: judgement of the appropriateness of the specific session objectives and their achievement to the overall achievement of objectives.

Strengths

Weaknesses

Overall grade: 1   2   3   4

Grade 1: The session fails to make an acceptable contribution to the attainment of the learning objective set.

Grade 2: The session makes an acceptable contribution to the attainment of the learning objectives, but significant improvement could be made.

Grade 3: The session makes a substantial contribution to the attainment of the learning objectives, but there is scope for improvement.

Grade 4: The session makes a full contribution to the attainment of the learning objectives